DISCARDED

THE BRAVE WOMEN
OF THE GULF WARS

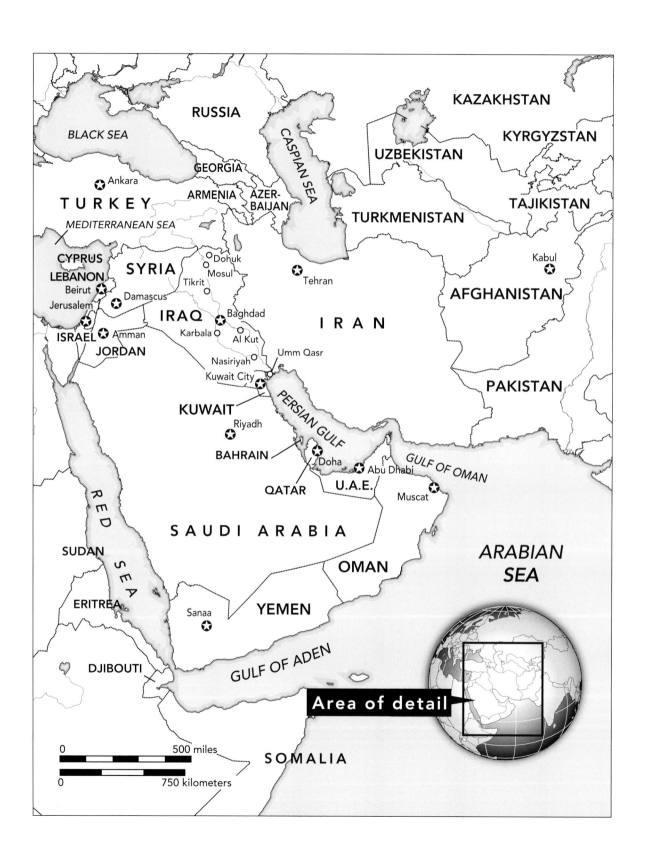

BLACK SEA

RUSSIA

CASPIAN SEA

KAZAKHSTAN

KYRGYZSTAN

UZBEKISTAN

GEORGIA

ARMENIA

AZER-
BAIJAN

TURKMENISTAN

TAJIKISTAN

⭐ Ankara

T U R K E Y

MEDITERRANEAN SEA

CYPRUS
LEBANON
Beirut ⭐

Damascus ⭐

Jerusalem

ISRAEL ⭐

Amman

JORDAN

SYRIA

○ Dohuk
○ Mosul
Tikrit ○

IRAQ

⭐ Baghdad

Karbala ○

○ Al Kut

Nasiriyah ○

Umm Qasr

Kuwait City

⭐ Tehran

I R A N

Kabul ⭐

AFGHANISTAN

PAKISTAN

KUWAIT

⭐ Riyadh

BAHRAIN

QATAR

PERSIAN GULF

Doha

Abu Dhabi

U.A.E.

GULF OF OMAN

⭐ Muscat

ARABIAN
SEA

RED SEA

SUDAN

ERITREA

Sanaa ⭐

S A U D I   A R A B I A

OMAN

YEMEN

DJIBOUTI

GULF OF ADEN

Area of detail

SOMALIA

0   500 miles

0   750 kilometers

THE BRAVE WOMEN
OF THE GULF WARS

OPERATION DESERT STORM
AND
OPERATION IRAQI FREEDOM

KAREN ZEINERT AND MARY MILLER

TWENTY-FIRST CENTURY BOOKS
MINNEAPOLIS

ACKNOWLEDGMENTS

Karen K. Zeinert (1940–2002) wishes to express appreciation to:
• the medical staffs at Appleton Memorial and University of Wisconsin Hospital and
Clinic for their most dedicated efforts to assist me in trying to defeat lymphoma;
• Carol and John in making my memorial service arrangements and all those
who attended thus making August 20 the most special of days; and
• Laura Walsh for her help and commitment in overseeing the Women at War series.

DEDICATION

To Lee Miller, for his encyclopedic knowledge of current events;
to Michael Hanson, for his generous offer to proofread my last-minute drafts;
and to Melody and Jack, for their patience while I was busy working on this book.
— *Mary Miller*

Interior Design by Ron Jaffe, Jaffe Enterprises

Cover photographs courtesy of Stephen Morton/Getty Images and Sgt. 1st Class William A. Jones/U. S. Army

PHOTOGRAPHS COURTESY OF:

Getty Images: pp. 6 (© Ian Waldie), 10 (© Carlo Allegri), 15 (© Bobbie Hernandez), 20 (© Scott Peterson), 31 (© Thomas S.
England/Time Life Pictures), 50 (© Scott Nelson), 61 (© Romeo Gacad/AFP), 76 (© Romeo Gacad/AFP), 96 (© Mario Tama), 99
(© Joseph Barrak/AFP); AP/Wide World Photos: pp. 8, 14, 19, 58, 65, 66; Corbis: pp. 24 (© Peter Turnley), 33 (© David Turnley),
41 (© Peter Turnley), 59 (© Dallas Morning News/Sygma), 71 (© David Turnley), 73, 83 (© David Turnley); Department of
Defense: pp. 27, 37, 69; Magnum: pp. 39 (© Abbas), 46-47 (© Susan Meiselas), 63 (© Paolo Pellegrin), 92 (© Thomas Dworzak);
Samuel S. Ferrell: p. 57; U. S. Army: p. 70; Richard Parry/WorldPictureNews: p. 88; CNN: p. 93

Map by Joe LeMonnier

Library of Congress Cataloging-in-Publication Data
Zeinert, Karen.
The brave women of the gulf wars: Operation Desert Storm
and Operation Iraqui Freedom/by Karen Zeinert and Mary Miller.
p. cm.
ISBN-13: 978-0-7613-2705-9 (lib. bdg.)
ISBN-10: 0-7613-2705-3 (lib. bdg.)
Summary: Traces the roots of the Persian Gulf War and the role women
played in the military, as correspondents, as medics, and on the homefront.
[1. Persian Gulf War, 1991—Women. 2. Operation Desert Shield, 1990-1991—
Women. 3. Persian Gulf War, 1991—Women. 4. Operation Desert Shield,
1990-1991—Women. 5. Women and the military. 6. Women and war.
7. United States—Armed Forces—Women.] I. Title.
DS79.744.W65 Z45 2006
956.70442'08 dc-21
2002014539

Twenty-First Century Books
A division of Lerner Publishing Group
241 First Avenue North
Minneapolis, Minnesota 55401 U.S.A.
Website address: www.lernerbooks.com

Manufactured in the United States of America
1 2 3 4 5 6 – JR – 11 10 09 08 07 06

CONTENTS

COURAGE UNDER FIRE

INTRODUCTION

" I am an American soldier, too. "
• **Private First Class Jessica Lynch**

The courage of military women in the Gulf conflict of 2003 was harshly tested only four days after the start of the war. On March 23, 2003, three female soldiers of the 507th Maintenance Company were thrust into the forefront of combat, where they showed resourcefulness, integrity, and courage under fire. The three female comrades-in-arms would meet dramatically different fates in the war. This is their story.

WOMEN OF THE 507TH

Private First Class Jessica Lynch, nineteen, and Private First Class Lori Piestewa, twenty-three, were roommates and army buddies. The young women first met at Fort Bliss, Texas, when they joined the 507th Maintenance Company. Supply clerk Lynch, who grew up in the small town of Palestine, West Virginia, joined the army to travel and to continue her education. She dreamed of one day becoming a kindergarten teacher.

Piestewa, a competitive softball player, was the divorced mother of a four-year-old boy and a three-year-old daughter. She grew up on an Indian

Private First Class Lori Piestewa (right) and Private First Class Jessica Lynch where they met in Fort Bliss, Texas, the day before their deployment to the Middle East

reservation near Tuba City, Arizona. She was proud to be one of the forty-eight Hopi Indians then serving in Iraq.

Specialist Shoshana Johnson, thirty, grew up in El Paso, Texas, in the shadow of an army base. The single mother of a two-year-old daughter, she joined the army to be a cook.

Both Piestewa and Johnson came from families with previous war experience. Piestewa's father had fought in Vietnam, and her grandfather had seen combat in World War II. Johnson's father, Claude, had served in the U.S. Army for twenty years. Her sister, Nikki, entered officer's training school at the start of the war. Her aunt is a former air force nurse, and two uncles and two cousins also serve in the military. On the day that Shoshana Johnson shipped out to Iraq, Claude spoke to his daughter as both a father and a fellow soldier: "I told her to keep her eyes open . . . be aware there is no 'battlefront.' . . . The enemy could be anywhere."[1] No one, including Claude Johnson, could have expected this small support unit to suffer one of the war's deadliest blows.

AMBUSH IN THE NIGHT

The job of the 507th Maintenance Company was to repair army vehicles and carry supplies. The unit followed the convoys of tanks and other armored vehicles traveling across the desert toward Baghdad, the capital of Iraq. The 507th was not a combat unit, but the soldiers were armed with weapons so that they could fight back if fired upon.

On the fourth day of the war, the 507th followed the 3rd Infantry Division as it pushed toward Baghdad. The line of tanks stretched for miles. The soldiers faced blinding sandstorms that caused the vehicles to break down frequently. In addition to limited visibility, the soldiers had difficulty negotiating through sandstorms because there are no landmarks in the desert.

The small support unit followed behind the convoy as it crossed through an area so dangerous that it would become known as "Ambush Alley." Due to faulty navigation, the 507th took a wrong turn while passing through the town of Nasiriyah. As the small supply unit approached the town, it was suddenly surrounded by Iraqi soldiers who fired at the Americans. The soldiers of the 507th tried to return fire, but many of their guns were jammed with sand and dust. The lightly armed unit didn't stand a chance. They had no other choice but to surrender.

WHERE IS THE 507TH?

Back home in Texas on Sunday morning, Claude Johnson was surfing the channels on the family's television set to find cartoons for his granddaughter Janelle. As he scanned the channels, he came across chilling news: Iraqi television was showing footage of five American prisoners of war. One of those POWs was his daughter—and Janelle's mother—Shoshana Johnson.

Johnson had been taken captive along with four other soldiers after the ambush of her unit near the city of Nasiriyah. She was the first American female POW since the "risk rule" was lifted in 1994.[2] (The lifting of this ban allowed women to take military positions in a war where there was the risk of being fired upon or taken captive.)

However, the 507th was a maintenance unit; its soldiers were not trained for battle. Although Johnson knew how to shoot an M-16 rifle in defense, she had joined the army to gain professional experience as a cook. Because maintenance units are not considered to be at high risk for capture, they don't receive special training in escape techniques or how to handle interrogations during captivity.

The image of a frightened Shoshana Johnson being interrogated by her Iraqi captors that was shown on American newscasts created outrage and fear back in the United States. It reignited the debate over the proper role of women on the battlefield. Although there was concern for all the POWs, the sight of a woman being held captive was especially upsetting to Americans back home. As Dinah Pokempner of Human Rights Watch observed: "Women had been at battle sites for a long

Specialist Shoshana Johnson being interrogated by her captors during her time as a prisoner of war

time, but usually as nurses rather than in combat. Americans are shocked at the sight of women POWs."[3]

Americans were worried about the treatment of the POWs for good reason. Many people remembered the accounts of torture suffered by U.S. and British POWs in the first Persian Gulf War in 1991. In that war, two women were held as POWs. Colonel Rhonda Cornum's helicopter had crashed on the last day of Gulf War I. Although she had survived the crash, she was taken prisoner by Iraqi soldiers. Both of her arms had been broken in the crash. Because of her injuries, she was unable to fight off a sexual attack by one of her captors.

WHERE ARE THE OTHERS?

As the families of the five POWs shown on television worried about the safety of their loved ones, the families of the other members of the 507th worried as well, but for different reasons. What had happened to the other nineteen soldiers? Had these soldiers been wounded or killed? Of this number, two women were listed as missing in action. Because the other soldiers of the 507th were not seen on television, their families began to fear the worst.

The Hopi tribal community joined together to support the family of Lori Piestewa. Reporters traveled to the small town of Palestine, West Virginia, to learn more about Jessica Lynch, the other female soldier who was missing. They were regaled with stories of a pint-sized teenager who was full of spirit. Wirt County High School coach Rodney Watson described the 5-foot-tall (150-cm) Lynch as "scrappy." He remembered: "She would do whatever it took to get the job done. She might have been small in stature, but she was big in heart."[4]

On the other side of the world from this small town, a dramatic turn of events was about to take place.

DRAMATIC RESCUE

On March 31, a thirty-two-year-old Iraqi lawyer named Mohammed Odeh al-Rehaief paid a visit to his wife at work. She was a nurse at Saddam Hospital in Nasiriyah. As he entered the hospital, Mohammed was surprised to see members of the Fedayeen roaming the hallways. (The most fierce and loyal of Saddam Hussein's soldiers, the Fedayeen also terrorized and tortured Iraqi citizens.)

Curious about their presence at the hospital, Mohammed discovered that they were guarding an American prisoner. He asked a friend who was a doctor at the hospital if he could see the American, but permission was denied. Mohammed's curiosity soon turned to dread when he looked through the window of the hospital room. He saw a tall Fedayeen dressed in black clothing slap a small woman back and forth across the face. Mohammed's heart went out to the young woman who was being mistreated. He made the fateful decision to help her.

To help this American woman, Mohammed needed to contact American soldiers. Despite extreme personal danger, he walked 6 miles (9.6 km) through a war zone until he found a U.S. Marine checkpoint. The soldiers were initially suspicious when Mohammed approached them. He told them that an American woman was being held prisoner at the hospital.

CIA (Central Intelligence Agency) agents on the ground near Nasiriyah confirmed Mohammed's information. They were now convinced that this woman was the missing soldier Jessica Lynch. The military alerted Special Operations to plan a rescue mission. They needed to know exactly where Lynch was being held captive and how many people were guarding her before they went in. The soldiers sent Mohammed back to the hospital on two separate trips to gain more information for the rescue attempt. Mohammed created maps of the hospital's layout for the soldiers. He reported that forty-one Fedayeen soldiers were standing watch at the hospital.

On one of his trips back to the hospital, Mohammed sneaked into Lynch's room. He reassured her that everything would be OK. At that point, all that was known about the extent of her injuries was that she had two broken legs. At the hospital, Mohammed overheard doctors planning to amputate one of her legs. Horrified, he was able to convince one of the doctors to delay the operation. Mohammed planned to stall the doctors until U.S. forces could rescue Lynch.

Mohammed's repeated trips to the hospital drew the attention of Iraqi authorities. They became suspicious of his actions and raided his house. Fearing for his safety, as well as the safety of his family, he went to the Americans for help. The Marines took Mohammed, his wife, and his six-year-old daughter into protective custody. They would later be moved to an undisclosed location near Washington, D.C.

On the night of April 1, nearly two weeks after the war had started and a little over a week since the 507th was ambushed, a daring rescue mission was launched under the cover of night. The special operations team was made up of marines, Army Rangers, Navy SEALs, and air services. To create a diversion, U.S. Marines attacked Iraqi forces in a Nasiriyah neighborhood. As the firefight raged on, electronic spy planes hovered over the hospital where Jessica Lynch was being held captive. Helicopters swooped in over the hospital from which commandos dropped down to the ground. Some of the commandos set up positions around the outside of the hospital to guard the rescue mission. The other commandos stormed the building.

Lynch had been hidden by her captors in a back corner of the emergency room. Without Mohammed's maps, the commandos might not have found her. As Lynch tried to hide by pulling a sheet over her head, the rescue team broke into the room. As she peeked out from under the covers, one of the commandos called: "Jessica Lynch, we're United States soldiers and we're here to protect you and take you home." As the soldier took off his helmet and approached her, Lynch replied: "I'm an American soldier, too."[5]

The commandos quickly bundled up Lynch and carried her down the stairs. An army doctor was waiting in a helicopter to tend to her injuries. As the helicopter became airborne, she begged him, "Don't let anybody leave me."[6] The U.S. Army had no intention of doing that. Lynch became the first POW to be successfully rescued from behind enemy lines since World War II.

Immediately after her rescue, Lynch was taken to a field hospital so that doctors could begin treating her injuries. Lynch had suffered a broken arm, two broken legs, a head wound, and a fractured disc in her spine. She was also weakened from surviving on a diet of orange juice and crackers. At that time, Lynch was unable to recall all the details from the ambush on her unit.

In the aftermath of Lynch's rescue, there was speculation in the media that the rescue operation was more combative than it needed to have been. Some news organizations, in particular the British Broadcasting Corporation (BBC), faulted the U.S. military for portraying the rescue mission as being more hero-

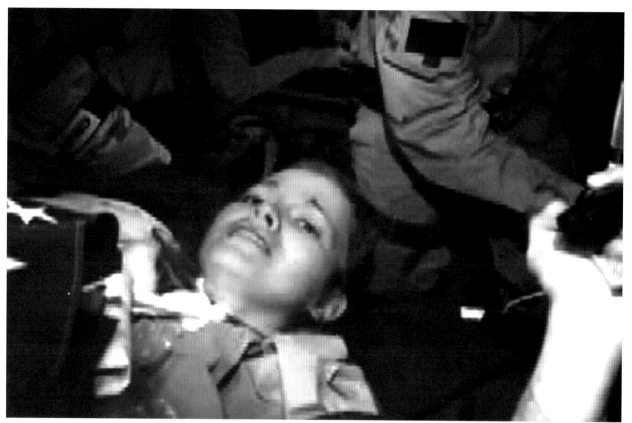

Lynch is carried on a stretcher during her rescue from Saddam Hospital on April 1, 2003, after being a prisoner of war for more than a week.

ic and dramatic than it was in reality. Spokespeople for the Pentagon called these allegations "void of all facts and absolutely ridiculous."[7]

In November 2003, Lynch agreed to be interviewed by Diane Sawyer for a television special. One reason that she agreed to the interview was to end speculation about her time in captivity. Lynch was now able to remember everything except the three hours from when the Humvee Lori Piestewa was driving crashed to the moment she woke up in an Iraqi hospital. Lynch is adamant that Piestewa and the other occupants of the vehicle fought bravely and died heroes. She also claims that media accounts of her fighting back during the ambush like a female Rambo are incorrect. She said that her gun had jammed and she spent the moments before the crash fearfully praying for her life. And while she is grateful for any assistance Mohammed might have contributed to her rescue effort, she does not remember him visiting her in the hospital or his accounts of her being slapped by a Fedayeen soldier.

Bittersweet News

The joy over the rescue of Jessica Lynch was bittersweet, because many soldiers of the 507th were either prisoners of war or still missing in action. Concern was mounting over the fate of these soldiers. Still, Lynch's rescue brought hope to the families of Lori Piestewa and Shoshana Johnson.

On the night they rescued Jessica Lynch, the soldiers discovered a shallow mass grave containing seven bodies and two bodies in the hospital morgue. The nine dead bodies were U.S. soldiers. As Lynch was being treated at an army hospital in Germany, the military began the sober task of identifying the bodies. For the Piestewa family, their worst fears had come true: One of the bodies was that of Private First Class Lori Piestewa. Six of the other bodies were her comrades from the 507th.

Piestewa, the young mother whose greatest worry as she shipped off to war was for the care of her children, was the first servicewoman to be killed in the line of duty in Operation Iraqi Freedom. She was also the first Native American to die in that battle. Piestewa had received severe head injuries in the Humvee crash and later died at the Iraqi hospital were Jessica Lynch was being held. Back in Tuba City, Arizona, the Hopi tribe mourned the loss of their "lady warrior" in tribal ceremonies. On April 11, the Army held a memorial service for the fallen members of the 507th. In an emotional ceremony, seven empty

SPC LORI A. PIESTEWA
14 DEC 79 - 23 MAR 03

This photo of Lori Piestewa was on display at the memorial ceremony held on April 11, 2003, in Fort Bliss, Texas, for the nine soldiers of the 507th Maintenance Company who were killed in the ambush.

helmets and seven empty pairs of combat boots lined the stage to symbolize the loss of these brave fighters.

THE WAITING GAME

As the Johnson family heard about the rescue of Jessica Lynch and the death of Lori Piestewa, they could only pray and wonder what had happened to Shoshana. Their worries grew when Iraqi television stopped showing footage of the American POWs. Did the lack of news mean that the POWs were already dead?

By April 12, twenty days after the ambush of the 507th, most large Iraqi cities, including Baghdad, had fallen. The last city to be taken over by coalition forces was Tikrit, the birthplace of Saddam Hussein. On April 13, the Marine 3rd Light Armored Reconnaissance Battalion headed toward Tikrit. As the Marines entered the city, they came across a group of Iraqi soldiers who had been abandoned by their superior officer. The Iraqis told the Marines that they knew where seven American POWs were being held.

The Marines followed the Iraqi soldiers to a small house. They stormed into the building to find seven American POWs—alive! Five were members of the 507th and two were helicopter pilots who had been listed as missing in action. Johnson was among this group. She had been shot in the foot during the ambush, but fortunately her injuries were not life-threatening.

The POWs told their story to the Marines. After the ambush of the 507th, the soldiers had been beaten by the villagers of Nasiriyah. They were then taken to Baghdad where they were interrogated. After that, they were treated surprisingly well. They were fed twice a day and given blankets. The Iraqis even operated on the POWs who needed medical care, including Johnson. For weeks, their Iraqi captors kept them on the run as they moved to different locations to escape the advancing coalition forces.

On April 16, twenty-five days after being taken prisoner in the ambush, the remaining members of the 507th, including Shoshana Johnson, were on their way home.

A TANGLED HISTORY

CHAPTER ONE

" If we let [Saddam] get away with this,
who knows what's going to be next? "
• **Lieutenant Jackie Jones**

The soldiers of the 507th became swept up with the rest of the U.S. military in political battles and conquests for power halfway around the world. To understand why U.S. soldiers were sent to Iraq in two separate wars within thirteen years of each other, one must look at the complex web of Middle East history. It is a history of centuries of turmoil and intrigue that—when added to the Western world's need for oil—led to the first Gulf War.

THE SANDS OF HISTORY RUN DEEP

Our civilization has its roots in the area now known as Iraq and Kuwait. The land between the Tigris and Euphrates Rivers was called Mesopotamia. This region is known as the Cradle of Civilization because it was the birthplace of various civilizations that moved humanity from prehistory to history.

Although this area is now known for its history of political turmoil, it also made important contributions to the world's literature, science, and religion. It is the birthplace of three major religions: Islam, Judaism, and Christianity. Little change occurred in the region until 1481, when Mesopotamia joined the Ottoman Empire. At one time, most of what is now known as the Middle East was part of the Ottoman Empire. When World War I broke out in 1914, this once powerful empire sided with Germany, Bulgaria, and Austria-Hungary. These countries were defeated by an alliance led by Great Britain, France, Russia, and the United States. When the war ended in 1918, Great Britain broke up the empire into independent countries.

In 1931 the nation of Iraq was established. Great Britain brought in a prince from the ruling Hashemite family in Jordan to rule Iraq. During World War II, Great Britain stepped in again to rule Iraq because many of the country's army officers tried to become allies of the Nazi party in Germany. After World War II ended in 1945, the British left Iraq in the hands of Hashemite royalty.

The reign of the royal family in Iraq was short-lived. In 1958 the Iraqi Army lined members of the royal family up against a wall and shot them. Although the army was in control of the country, it faced challenges from the nationalist Baath party. This political party wanted to overthrow all monarchies in the region and unite all Arabs—from Iraq to Morocco. The party's goal was to create a single, powerful Arab state.[1] This goal was never fulfilled.

The Baath party often dealt harshly with people who did not share its goals. In 1968 the Baath party gained control of the Iraqi Army and Iraq. Second in command of the Iraqi Baath party was a thirty-one-year-old named Saddam Hussein.

Although the history of the Middle East has been marked with violence, Saddam Hussein introduced a new level of brutality. Known as the "Butcher of Baghdad" because of his cruelty toward enemies, he performed his first assassination at age fifteen. As a young man, Hussein served in various positions, each one more influential than the last, in the Baath party. To gain the most powerful political position in Iraq, Hussein pushed aside the current leader who was also his cousin, Ahmad Hassan al-Bakr, and made himself president. In order to eliminate any opposition from his cousin, Hussein put him in prison, where he remained until he died in 1982.

When Hussein seized power in 1979, Iraq was a prosperous, oil-rich country. After twenty-five years of his rule, it would become a debt-ridden country whose residents lived in extreme poverty. While the Iraqi citizens lived in squalor, Hussein lived in luxury. In a desert country desperate for clean drinking water, Hussein had swimming pools and fountains built at his twenty opulent palaces. Hussein was able to steal Iraq's wealth because the citizens were too terrified to resist. He used torture and intimidation to keep the people in line.

MODERN IRAQ

With a population of more than 20 million people, present-day Iraq covers an area of about 169,000 square miles (438,000 sq km). Geographically, Iraq is surrounded by Iran to the east, Turkey to the north, Saudi Arabia and Kuwait to the south, and Syria and Jordan to the west. Saudi Arabia, which has the world's largest proven oil reserves, is a powerful neighbor.

Some 60 percent of Iraqis are Shiite Muslims. Despite their large numbers, they have never held much power in the country. Living mostly in the rural south and east of Iraq, they have long faced discrimination from the Sunni Arabs.

Although they are only 20 percent of the population of Iraq, Sunni Arabs dominate the religion of Islam worldwide. They gained their dominance in Iraq because Saddam Hussein is a Sunni Muslim, as are his government and military leaders. The rift between Shiite and Sunni Muslims occurred about fourteen centuries ago. The Shiites broke away from the Sunni majority because of a disagreement over who should follow the Prophet Muhammad as the spiritual leader of Islam. The Sunni Muslims believed that the leader should be one of the senior members of the faith, while the Shiite Muslims demanded that only a person with a direct bloodline connection to Muhammad could fill this position.[2]

Saddam Hussein appearing on Iraqi television on March 20, 2003

This Kurdish rebel in northern Iraq is in training to help the United States oppose Saddam Hussein's regime before the second Gulf War began.

The Kurds, on the other hand, live in the rugged, northern part of Iraq. This group makes up the remainder of the Iraqi population, at 20 percent. In 1988 the Kurds felt Hussein's wrath when he used chemical gas on the town of Halabja. This act is often pointed to as an example of Hussein's willingness to use chemical weapons of mass destruction.

BORDER WARS

Although Iraq and Kuwait were independent countries by 1920, Kuwait was continuously forced to defend its borders. In the late 1930s the king of Iraq tried to claim that Kuwait belonged to Iraq. Part of Kuwait's value lay in the discovery of oil in that region. In 1958, after the Iraqi military led a violent coup against the monarchy, the new military leaders also tried to claim Kuwait. When Kuwait gained its independence from Great Britain in 1961, Iraq tried to step in and take over its smaller neighbor. Britain sent troops to the area to prevent the takeover. Eventually, though, Iraq agreed to give up all claims to Kuwait in exchange for $84 million.

Tensions continued to simmer between the neighboring countries. In 1973 armed conflicts broke out along their borders. The issue was no longer over national boundaries, but oil. Whoever controlled the region would also control most of the world's oil supply. By the 1980s, Kuwait had strengthened its defenses and taken over its oil reserves from British control. It had become one of the world's richest countries.

In August 1980, Hussein began a bloody eight-year war with Iraq's neighbor to the east, Iran. It was during this war that Saddam Hussein violated international law and used poison gas against Iranian soldiers.[3]

The Iran-Iraq War ended with a cease-fire in July 1988. Although Iraq suffered far fewer casualties than Iran, it had borrowed more money to fund the war. The country was now deeply in debt. Hussein demanded that Kuwait cancel his debt of $17 billion, which he had borrowed to fund the war against Iran. That money had made it possible for Hussein to train and equip one million soldiers. Only the United States, the Soviet Union, and China had larger armies. Hussein also decided to drive up the price of oil to replace the money spent on the war. To increase the price of oil, he planned to slow down production in the Rumalia oil field, which Iraq shared with Kuwait.

Kuwait refused to ignore the debt or to slow down their oil production. Hussein then accused Kuwait of slanting its drills so that it could pump oil from the Iraqi side of the border.

Hussein eventually decided that he could solve most of his problems by annexing Kuwait, or declaring it a part of Iraq. Kuwait had vast gold reserves in its banks as well as in accounts overseas. For instance, the emir (prince) alone had more than $130 billion in foreign investments. Hussein believed that if he governed Kuwait, he could cancel his debts, raid Kuwait's bank accounts, and control the country's output of oil, which could possibly drive prices upward again.

Hussein began to assess the international risks he faced if his army invaded Kuwait. He clearly had the means to conquer the country and install a puppet government. The main difficulty, he believed, was the reaction of foreign nations. Would they come to Kuwait's aid?

U.S. Support for Kuwait

One of the countries Hussein was most concerned about was the United States. When American intelligence officials noticed a large number of Iraqi troops massing near the Iraqi-Kuwaiti border, they became uneasy. Several American officials went to Iraq to speak with its leader. Hussein convinced them that all was well. Reports about threats he had made were greatly exaggerated, he said; journalists were simply painting an unfair picture of him.

On July 25, Hussein requested a meeting with April C. Glaspie, the U.S. ambassador to Iraq. What was said during this meeting will forever be in question. The Iraqis declared that Glaspie said the United States saw the dispute between Iraq and Kuwait as a matter to be resolved between the two countries; America would not become involved. Glaspie insisted she told Hussein that the United States did not have a treaty with Kuwait pledging support if it was attacked. She made clear, however, that: "We would support our friends in the Gulf, we would defend their sovereignty and integrity. . . . We would insist on settlements being made in a nonviolent manner, not by threats, not by intimidation, and certainly not by aggression."[4] These comments did not appear in the official transcript prepared by the Iraqis.

Believing he was safe to do so, Hussein ordered his troops to invade eight days later. As they poured into Kuwait, an unprepared world could do little but watch. But when some of these same troops began to gather on the Kuwaiti–Saudi Arabian border that same day, world leaders shook off their shock and mentally drew a line in the sand.

Invasion of Kuwait

In the early hours of August 2, 1990, more than 100,000 heavily armed Iraqi soldiers marched into Kuwait. The invaders overwhelmed the Kuwaitis and their tiny army of 20,000 soldiers. The Iraqi soldiers were able to race along six-lane superhighways toward the Persian Gulf without much opposition. Nine hours after the Iraqis had crossed the border, they controlled most of Kuwait and all of Kuwait City, the capital. By invading Kuwait, Hussein not only would gain that country's oil supply but also have the potential to control global oil prices.[5]

One of the reasons the Kuwaitis were taken by surprise was that even though serious differences had long existed between Kuwait and Iraq, the two countries had been able to settle their disagreements by negotiation, without waging all-out war. The two countries had even scheduled a meeting to discuss the latest disputes over oil production and the shared Rumalia oil field. As a result, most people in Kuwait thought that war with Iraq was highly unlikely.

Believing they were secure, many in Kuwait reacted to the first signs of an invasion with little concern. Jadranka Porter, a writer from Yugoslavia who lived in the capital, actually ignored the sound of gunshots. Afterward, trying to explain her lack of anxiety, she said: "It was a different kind of gunfire which half-woke me at about 5:30 A.M. on Thursday August 2, 1990. It did not fully register at the time and sounded something like thunder in the distance. I turned over and went back to sleep."[6]

At 6:00 A.M., friends called Porter to warn her that Iraq had invaded. They insisted that they had seen tanks and trucks moving at breakneck speed toward her city and that she should take precautions. She went outside, where she joined a growing throng of anxious neighbors, who had likewise been warned. Later, describing an alarming scene, Porter said:

> *[Around 7:00 A.M.] we saw the first tanks rolling past the intersection. . . . I counted dozens of them. They were followed by scores of trucks carrying troops in combat gear, with water and gasoline tankers coming up behind. And then the helicopters arrived. They came roaring over our heads in groups of three and four and five. They made a tremendous racket and were like swarms of hornets. . . . We had no guns and my main thought was: How are we going to save ourselves?[7]*

Other foreigners who lived and worked in Kuwait, about one million people, also wondered how they were going to save themselves, for Iraqi soldiers had not treated their victims kindly in the past.

Kuwait's 600,000 citizens didn't feel any safer. Unlike the emir of Kuwait, Sheik Jaber al-Ahmed al-Sabah, and most of his family, few Kuwaitis had received a timely warning that would have enabled them to flee to neighboring Saudi Arabia. Many of these citizens, especially government officials, were afraid for their lives, and their fear was justified. When they seized the palace, Iraqi soldiers killed the sheik's brother before he had a chance to flee. The soldiers had orders to assassinate the emir if they captured him. They also had long lists of names of so-called enemies of Iraq. Many of these people were arrested and never heard from again.

While the Kuwaitis wrestled with the issue of how best to stay alive, world leaders and Kuwait's emir struggled with the question of how best to deal with Saddam Hussein.

Many Kuwaiti women and children became refugees as they fled their country .

OPERATION DESERT SHIELD

While Iraqi troops eyed Saudi Arabia, world leaders reacted to Saddam Hussein's invasion. In the evening hours of August 2, 1990, the same day that Iraq invaded Kuwait, the United Nations (UN) Security Council held an emergency meeting and quickly passed Resolution 660. The resolution condemned the attack and demanded the immediate withdrawal of Iraqi soldiers from Kuwaiti soil.

The following day, the League of Arab Nations also condemned the attack. The league demanded not only that Hussein withdraw his troops but also, alarmed by a possible attack on Saudi Arabia, warned him not to advance on another nation.

At the same time, many countries began to take action on their own. If Kuwaitis or the Kuwaiti government had investments or bank accounts in their country, officials froze the funds so that Hussein could not plunder them. Other nations announced an embargo; they would no longer buy products from Iraq, nor would they sell anything to Hussein until he withdrew his troops from Kuwait.

When the invasion occurred, several world leaders, including Margaret Thatcher, prime minister of Great Britain, and George H. W. Bush, president of the United States, were attending a political conference in Aspen, Colorado. As soon as Thatcher heard about the invasion, she consulted with Bush about how best to convince Hussein to leave Kuwait. Because the League of Arab Nations had asked for time to try to find a local solution to the problem, both leaders agreed to wait until league members had done their best to persuade Hussein to withdraw his troops before taking action.

When it became clear that the league could not solve the problem alone and that Iraq would not withdraw without pressure to do so, Thatcher urged the UN to organize a worldwide embargo. The Security Council agreed with Thatcher. On August 6 it passed Resolution 661, which asked all nations to stop trading with Iraq. Saddam Hussein reacted by annexing Kuwait.

While the world waited for the embargo to go into effect, Prime Minister Thatcher and President Bush became deeply concerned for the safety of Saudi

Arabia. But they couldn't just send troops to the country; they had to be asked to do so.

At first Saudi Arabia refused to believe that it was in imminent danger. Also, it did not want to appear to be under the influence of Western nations. In the eyes of many Middle Easterners, especially fundamental Muslims, Westerners (and most particularly Americans) are part of an immoral culture. To invite "infidels" into one's country where holy shrines are located was touchy at best. But as the number of Iraqis, clearly prepared for battle, increased at the border, the rulers of Saudi Arabia realized that they were in peril. Shortly after, they issued an invitation to foreign governments for help.

To avoid the issue of Saudi Arabia being under the influence of Western nations, British and American diplomats worked hard to build an international coalition. Called Operation Desert Shield, more than forty nations eventually contributed 700,000 troops, 1,600 combat aircraft, and almost 200 warships, as well as medical teams and money. The stated purpose of Operation Desert Shield was to defend Saudi Arabia and force Iraq to withdraw from Kuwait.

Among the 700,000 troops were more than 400,000 Americans, the first of whom began to arrive in Saudi Arabia on August 9, 1990. These troops eventually included 40,000 women, whose presence created unique problems. The role played by females in Saudi Arabian culture was very restricted. For example, women could not go out in public without being accompanied by a male relative. Also, all Saudi women had to be draped in clothing that completely covered all but their eyes while in public. Saudi leaders, fearing the influence American women might have on their nation's women, did not want them to enter the country.

However, since American women were so much a part of the military in 1990, it was not practical to leave them home. Compromises were finally worked out, but this didn't eliminate the problem altogether. Although female soldiers bristled at the idea, they agreed to be escorted by men when they left the base. But while they were working, they refused to do anything differently than they would in the United States. So when it got warm, women took off their jackets, even though Saudis gasped when they did so. These shameless hussies, Saudis said, were disrobing in public. Others called U.S. military headquarters to regis-

Female military personnel take part in a discussion in preparation for deployment to Saudi Arabia during Operation Desert Shield.

ter their anger when they saw American women driving trucks or piloting planes; Saudi women weren't allowed to drive anything, not even a car.

Shortly after foreign troops began to arrive in Saudi Arabia, Hussein's soldiers started to round up people from coalition nations who were living or visiting in Kuwait when the invasion took place. Soldiers went door to door to try to find at least 4,000 British and 2,500 American citizens. Saddam Hussein then announced he would place male hostages at sites that coalition troops might target. In short, he planned to use the men as human shields. This caused an international uproar.

To quell the protest, Hussein appeared on Iraqi television on August 23 with fifteen hostages. He planned to portray the hostages as "guests" rather than captives. But Hussein's public-relations gimmick failed miserably. All of the so-called guests, despite their orders to smile, appeared ill at ease. Instead of being confident about the well-being of the captives, especially the children, onlookers were more alarmed than ever. They believed that Hussein might use all of the hostages as human shields. The outrage that followed the broadcast was so great that Hussein decided to release all women and children five days later.

Saddam Hussein then turned his attention from using hostages as shields to trying to break up the coalition. First, he threatened massive resistance to anyone who might attack him. Next he targeted environmentalists by threatening an ecological disaster. If coalition troops so much as looked like they would enter Kuwait, he vowed to set every oil well in Kuwait ablaze and pour crude oil into the Persian Gulf. (Hussein later made good on these promises. On January 25, his men poured crude oil into the Gulf, and on February 23 they set approximately 700 oil wells on fire.)

His most serious threat to the coalition, though, was his renewed vow to attack Israel. This nation was to be a home for both native Palestinians and Jews who migrated to the Middle East in large numbers in the 1930s and 1940s to escape persecution. After the British withdrew in 1948, fighting broke out between the Jews and Palestinians over who would rule the land. Hussein believed that if he attacked Israel, many Arabs would have found it impossible to defend an old enemy; instead, he thought they would withdraw from the coalition, severely weakening it.

While Hussein shook his fist and made threats, diplomats continued to shore up the coalition, reminding them that buckling under now would be a mistake. Finally, on November 29, 1990, Resolution 678 was passed. It authorized the coalition to use force to drive Hussein out of Kuwait. A battle royal—known as Operation Desert Storm—was in the making.

OPERATION DESERT STORM

CHAPTER TWO

""This is the moment everyone trains for.""

• **Captain Stephanie Wells, U.S. Air Force pilot**

American women have served in the armed forces at every opportunity in our nation's history. But in the early years, the first female soldiers had little choice but to enlist in disguise. These women often passed themselves off as young men who had not yet begun to shave. Sally St. Clair, who fought in the Revolutionary War (1775–1783), was one of America's first female soldiers. She died on the battlefield. During the Civil War (1861–1865) about four hundred women fought, again in trousers and shirts.

In the 1900s, women struggled for the right to serve their country in wartime without having to pretend they were men. During America's participation in World War I (1917–1918), thousands of female office workers clamored to enlist as support personnel.

Although women proved their worth to the services in World War I, when World War II (1939–1945) loomed on the horizon, they once again struggled for the right to serve their country. In 1941, Edith Nourse Rogers, a congresswoman from Massachusetts, introduced a bill in the House of Representatives to form the Women's Army Auxiliary Corps (WAAC). This bill was so controversial that ninety-six representatives and thirty-one senators refused to vote on it. It became law because of strong support from the Army's chief of staff and the secretary of war who influenced the House of Representatives and Senate to pass the bill. By the end of the war, 30,000 females had served in the corps. They filled positions that ran the gamut from typists to air-traffic controllers. The Navy, Marines, and Coast Guard followed the Army's example, accepting women for a variety of openings when a manpower shortage occurred.

Once again, women proved they were invaluable. So when a bill came up in Congress in 1948 that would allow women to become a permanent part of the armed services, there was little serious opposition. However, women were still forbidden from serving on Navy ships or on Air Force combat planes.

Although it took years to do so, by the time the United States was deeply mired in a war in Vietnam (1957–1975), women had become an integral part of the armed services. However, because the war in Vietnam was fought mainly against guerrillas in the jungle rather than on a typical battlefield, leaders of the armed services at first refused to send women to Asia. There was, the men said, no relatively safe place to assign them as there had been in previous wars.

Enlisted women, reflecting the growing role women were playing in society, refused to take no for an answer. After heated arguments, the armed services finally relented. At least 7,500 female specialists served in Vietnam with the U.S. military, mostly with the Army Nurse Corps or the Navy Nurses Corps. Although the majority of women served as nurses and medics, some women also worked as air-traffic controllers, intelligence officers, technicians, and security personnel. Eight Army nurses and one Air Force nurse lost their lives in the Vietnam War. These brave women opened the door for modern female soldiers—the brave women of the Gulf Wars.

WOMEN IN OPERATION DESERT STORM

Within hours after Saddam Hussein had marched into Kuwait on August 2, 1990, U.S. armed forces were put on alert. By January 1991, more than 400,000 U.S. troops had been deployed in the Middle East.[1] A total of 37,000 military personnel were women. Although many came from National

Guard units, about 26,000 were in the Army, 3,700 were in the Navy, 2,200 were in the Marines, and 5,300 in the Air Force. Thirteen women were in the Coast Guard.[2]

This was the first war waged by all-volunteer military forces. The draft was not used for Operation Desert Storm. Also, female soldiers played a much more active role in combat than in any previous war. On September 5, 1990, the first combined force of American men and women ever to ship out in wartime conditions left San Diego for the Persian Gulf. Of the 1,260 on the *U.S.S. Acadia*, 360 were women.[3]

As in all previous wars, the role women would play in Operation Desert Storm, also known as the Persian Gulf War, was open to debate. But since women

Army medic Holly Valance hugs her seven-week-old baby, Cheyenne, before going off to the Gulf crisis. Photographs like these intensified the debates about sending women into dangerous positions during war.

accounted for 11 percent of active soldiers and 15 percent of the reserves, even critics who opposed sending women to war admitted that they had to be included. After all, how could the services leave behind specialists—women who were supply experts, ammunition technicians, brigade commanders, helicopter pilots, and members of combat support teams—whose skills and knowledge would be needed?

What made this debate more emotional than it had been in the past was that many of those who would be sent overseas were married women—careerists in the military or reservists finishing their long enlistment—who had children. The thought of sending women into dangerous positions deeply upset some Americans; sending mothers into danger upset them even more. As the debate intensified, heart-wrenching photos of crying children waving good-bye to teary-eyed mothers assigned to the Gulf region dominated the news. This caused deep resentment on the part of many parents in the military. Fathers believed that their pain in being separated from their children was just as great as a mother's pain, and it was ignored; mothers resented being portrayed as overly emotional.

Critics opposed to sending women to the Middle East also argued that the desert was no place for females. Women simply pointed out that if enlisted women had managed to survive near the fronts in Europe during World War II and the jungles of Asia during the Vietnam War, this generation of females could serve in the deserts of the Middle East.

What both male and female soldiers endured was every bit as difficult as critics said it would be. Temperatures could easily reach 100°F (38°C) during the day and fall below freezing at night. In addition, the air was extremely dry, parching skin and making breathing difficult. And then there were sandstorms. One female recruit recalled:

> The sandstorms scrubbed the paint off the sides of the trucks and made it hard to breathe and even harder to see. The rains when they did come came down so hard you couldn't see ten feet in front of your face. . . . The sand fleas, the rats that always seemed to be running around the tents, the spiders the size of dinner plates that could jump five feet in the air, all this added to my [discomfort].[4]

In previous wars women had served mostly as nurses and administrative staff. Persian Gulf War I was the first war in which the majority of female serv-

These soldiers were based in the Persian Gulf during Desert Shield and Desert Storm. Dawn Dorsch (left) was a private for a special operations support battalion. The rose she holds is for her fiancé. The soldier on the right is unidentified.

ice personnel were not nurses. It was the first time that men and women served together in integrated units in a war zone.

In past wars, women had served far from the front lines, which were considered the most dangerous. During the Gulf War, however, the rear lines were no longer safe. The Iraqis often fired Scud missiles into the supply and ammunition areas, which were well behind the front lines. The Iraqis' ability to hit targets well behind the front lines blurred the distinction between combat and noncombat areas. This turn of events helped to expand the areas where women were allowed to serve. Fourteen women who served in Gulf War I received combat awards for crossing minefields during the ground war or for receiving and returning enemy fire.[5]

SCUDBUSTERS, PILOTS, AND SPECIAL AGENTS

Desert Storm had two phases. The first phase was a massive air attack. Beginning on January 17, 1991, coalition aircraft weakened Hussein's ability to fight by bombing military equipment and bases in Iraq. The second phase was a ground offensive that lasted from February 24 to February 28. After pretending to attack from one direction, ground troops entered the southernmost tip of Iraq from Saudi Arabia on February 24, then marched toward Kuwait. Women played many important roles in both stages of the war.

Some, like Deborah Sheehan, constructed shelters. A crane operator, Sheehan helped build a hospital for some of the estimated 10,000 to 20,000 casualties expected during the conflict. Although Sheehan was not involved in combat, she was still in danger. "What we were offloading," she said, "was ammo, vehicles, tents, supplies for the fleet hospital at Al Jubayl. . . . While on the pier, we were under attack by Scuds [Iraqi missiles]. One blew up over the warehouse while we were unloading some ammo."[6]

The Iraqi Army had hundreds of Scud missiles left over from its war with Iran, and as soon as it became clear that coalition forces were going to use force to drive Iraqi troops from Kuwait, Hussein's men began to fire away. These surface-to-surface missiles were a real threat. Not only did Scuds have powerful warheads that could be hurled through the air for 500 miles (805 km), but they could be used also to deliver deadly chemicals, which Hussein had repeatedly threatened to do. Because the missiles were launched from flatbed trucks that were moved about, it was almost impossible for coalition forces to pinpoint and destroy the launching sites. Instead, coalition forces worked on destroying the missiles while they were in the air. This was usually done with the help of Patriot missiles. The soldiers who shot down Scuds were called "Scudbusters."

Lieutenant Phoebe Jeter became the first female Scudbuster in the Gulf War. She commanded the all-male unit Patriot Delta Battery near Riyadh, the

MARIE THERESE ROSSI

MAJOR, UNITED STATES ARMY

Major Marie T. Rossi was one of the first women to participate in Desert Storm when she led her squadron of ammunition-laden helicopters into Iraq on February 24, 1991. She was also one of thirteen women who died during the conflict. On March 1, 1991, the helicopter she was piloting crashed into an unmarked tower during bad weather.

Shortly before the ground war began, Rossi was interviewed on national television about the role women would play in this conflict. Rossi downplayed her part. "What I am doing," she said, "is no greater or no less than the man who is flying next to me. Or in back of me. . . . Personally, as an aviator and a soldier, this is the moment that everybody trains for—that I've trained for—so I feel ready to meet a challenge.[7]

Many Americans had seen Rossi's interview, and it brought the war closer to home for them. One woman said: "When I saw her on television it made the war seem personal to me. . . . Prior to that, I didn't know anybody over there. Now I felt I knew her."[8] *As a result, the announcement of Rossi's death, again on national television, saddened many viewers. Major Rossi was buried in Arlington National Cemetery on March 11, 1991, with full military honors, including a twenty-one gun salute.*

capital of Saudi Arabia—one of Iraq's favorite targets. On January 21, Jeter heard the sirens go off, which meant that Scuds were headed in her direction. After hearing the warning, she had eight minutes to destroy the missiles before they would hit the ground. Donning gas masks just in case the Scuds had chemical warheads, Jeter and her assistants immediately began to analyze information concerning the speed of the weapons and their probable paths. She then gave her assistant the information he needed to launch missiles to destroy Scuds in midair.

While Jeter was shooting down Scuds, women pilots were delivering goods to the troops. For example, Major Marie T. Rossi led a squadron of Chinook helicopters (large cargo-carrying aircraft) loaded with ammunition during the first ground assault. Captain Ann Weaver Worster flew a KC-135 tanker. Tankers refueled fighter aircraft in midair.

Lieutenant Kelly Franke flew 105 combat-support missions during Desert Storm. She transported troops, brought back prisoners of war, and delivered ammunition and equipment to the war zone. She also rescued an injured navy diver under very difficult conditions. Franke hovered her helicopter 75 feet (23 m) above the water in a strong wind while her crew pulled the diver from the water.

Captain Stephanie Wells was part of the largest airlift operation in history. She flew twenty-two flights during the war, transporting helicopters, trucks, tanks, Patriot missiles, medical supplies, and some troops.

Many women were also responsible for supporting invading coalition troops. Fuel, water, and ammunition had to be brought to tanks, trucks, and soldiers as they advanced through the desert. Captain Cynthia Mosley commanded a supply battalion. She and one hundred men and women in her unit followed the troops as they penetrated deep into Iraqi territory, pulling up beside tanks and trucks to refuel them so they could continue on their way.

Delivering supplies in enemy territory was dangerous. Specialists Melissa Rathbun-Nealy and David Lockett drove a twenty-five-wheel truck loaded with tanks. When they got stuck in the sand, Hussein's troops moved in on them. Both Rathbun-Nealy and Lockett were wounded before being taken prisoner. Rathbun-Nealy was the first female prisoner of war taken during Desert Storm.

While Rathbun-Nealy and her partner were under Iraqi guard, American female soldiers were guarding Iraqi prisoners of war in Saudi Arabia. At first, women were assigned to the less dangerous jobs at the prison, answering phones and filing records. Several women bristled at the restrictions, and one, who had worked in a maximum-security prison at home, insisted that she be assigned full guard duties. She had, she said, seen tougher prisoners in the United States than in the Middle East. Another, Sergeant Kitty Bussell, was denied access to the prisoners during a riot. She had been trained in riot control and was well armed. Bussell patted her rifle, told the male guard, "I'm as good a shot as anybody," and then charged in to do her job.[9]

Women also played a part in dangerous secret operations. Sergeant Theresa Lynn Treloar served in a unit that put her closer to the battlefront than any other American woman during the war. Her mission was so secret that army

Specialist Melissa Rathbun-Nealy was the first female to be taken as a prisoner of war during Desert Storm. Here, she holds a copy of a newspaper article about her capture while being transported for treatment on the hospital ship U.S.N.S. Mercy.

officials not only refuse to describe it years after the event, but also refuse to allow any photographs of Treloar to be published. When a reporter interviewing Sergeant Treloar worried about the dangers she faced, Treloar emphasized the fact that she wanted to be part of this special unit. "I chose this," she said, "and I knew what I was getting myself into when I chose it."[10] During her mission, she carried a rifle, a light antitank weapon, a sidearm, and a grenade to protect herself and the other members of her unit. In short, she was not to be taken lightly by the enemy.

The builders, pilots, suppliers, guards, special agents, and the thousands of other women who served in Desert Storm took great pride in what they accomplished during the war. These accomplishments came with a price, though:

Thirteen women died during the war, and twenty-one were wounded in action. Still, one of the most startling lessons learned from the conflict was the public's acceptance of women in the military. Pete Williams, spokesman for the secretary of defense said: "One of the lessons we've learned from . . . Desert Storm is the extent to which the nation accepted the significant role of women in the operation. Until then, there had always been a concern that having women involved in combat would be traumatic for the country."[11] It was a statement that would have warmed the hearts of all military women who had paved the way for the women of Desert Storm.

After the Storm

Americans were elated when Desert Storm ended as quickly and successfully as it did. For the U.S. troops, there were only 148 battle-related deaths and less than 500 wounded men and women, many of whom were expected to recover fully. (In contrast, the Iraqis suffered at least 20,000 casualties. The coalition, including figures for U.S. troops, reported 1,000.) The United States was in the mood to celebrate. American flags were hoisted high in the air, patriotic songs dominated the airwaves, and huge parades were organized to welcome home the conquering heroes.

Later, Americans began to realize that all was not well. Some were disheartened that Saddam Hussein was still in power. Even though the UN resolution did not authorize an invasion of Iraq, a number of people thought that the coalition should have pushed on to Baghdad to put an end to Hussein's political career once and for all. Hussein was still a serious threat to the region.

Furthermore, Hussein was proving to be very difficult at the negotiating table. The coalition demanded that Iraq pay for the damages it had caused in Kuwait, destroy its chemical and biological weapons, and end any plans to develop a nuclear weapons program. The coalition wanted international inspectors to enter Iraq and verify that Hussein had fulfilled these demands. Hussein flat-out refused to accept even one of these conditions. His soldiers had withdrawn from Kuwait, he argued, and that was enough.

A soldier of the U.S. liberation forces in Kuwait City talks to a Kuwaiti woman after the end of Operation Desert Storm.

To pressure him into becoming a bit more cooperative, the UN decided to continue its embargo. Soon, stories about starving Iraqi children and sick men and women who were dying for lack of medicine began to draw international attention. The embargo was modified to allow Iraq to sell some of its oil to raise funds for food and medical supplies.

Americans were also distressed when two revolts in Iraq, which were direct results of the war, ended in disaster. Believing that Hussein had been seriously weakened by the conflict and hoping they would get help from the coalition,

Shiites in southern Iraq and Kurds in northern Iraq decided to rebel. But coalition members did not rush to their defense. The coalition feared that Hussein's demise would lead to more bloody battles as various groups struggled for control of the country.

The most the coalition would do was enforce a no-fly zone regulation in southern Iraq. Established at the end of the war, it was originally intended to protect the Kuwaitis and Saudi Arabians from Iraqi air attacks. Hussein complained about this zone, and another one that was established in the north to protect the Kurds, but he did not have the power to stop coalition aircraft from patrolling the area. Even though he couldn't use his aircraft, Hussein's troops had little trouble crushing the rebellions.

Although everyone in Iraq and Kuwait experienced the trauma of war and its aftermath, women in these nations faced additional challenges. When Hussein invaded Kuwait, almost half the teachers and dentists and one third of the doctors in Iraq were females. In fact, there were only a few professions and organizations, including the armed forces, that didn't accept women. Hussein encouraged women in the workforce because the country lacked workers. But after the Gulf War, Iraq was deeply in debt and unable to sell its oil. Hussein ordered women to stay home so that men could have the few available jobs.

Hussein passed laws that made it illegal for women to work. Some of the unemployed were war widows who had to support their families. When some two hundred women turned to prostitution to earn enough money to buy food, they were arrested and publicly beheaded.

The women of Kuwait were also affected by the aftermath of the war, but in a very different way. When the emir Sheikh Jaber al-Ahmed al-Sabah reinstated Kuwait's parliament, women clamored for the right to vote. This is a new Kuwait, they argued, with new rules. Pointing to their role in resisting Iraqi occupation and using some of the demonstration techniques they had developed during the war, women drew attention to their cause. Finally, in 1999, the emir issued a royal decree granting women the right to cast a ballot. Parliament rejected the decree, 32 to 30.

Although Kuwaiti women hold many prominent appointed positions—for example, president of Kuwait University—they still cannot vote. Women are

After Desert Storm, Iraqi women mourned the loss of loved ones and tried to deal with the trauma of war.

also banned from holding elective office. Despite their determination to gain suffrage, Kuwaiti women were still unable to vote in 2004.

DEBATE OVER WOMEN IN COMBAT

A major issue for American women after the first Gulf War was the debate about females serving in combat. Supporters of this issue were elated by the role that women had successfully played in the war. They argued that now was the time to repeal all laws forbidding women from holding positions that might involve them in combat. Americans had seen television reports about women in camouflage whose abilities seemed endless, and they were inclined, supporters believed, to let women volunteer for combat positions.

Congresswoman Patricia Schroeder spearheaded the drive in the House of Representatives. To back her cause, she used the recommendation of the powerful board of the Defense Department Advisory Committee on Women in the Services (DACOWITS). This board, made up of approximately thirty-five civilians who are outstanding in their fields—for example, education, law, business—is appointed by the secretary of defense to give advice about women's issues in the military. After listening to military advisers and reviewing the role that women had played in the war, the DACOWITS board voted 29 to 4 to recommend that females should be allowed to become combatants.

When this recommendation was presented to the membership of DACOWITS, approximately three hundred men and women, the audience broke into cheers. Many, including Jeanne Holm, a retired Air Force major general, believed that this would pave the way for women to reach the highest positions in the armed services. Some women in the military thought that they were denied promotions because they hadn't participated in combat. Holm spoke for them when she said, "It [combat experience] is the linchpin for everything else."[12]

When Schroeder heard about the board's recommendation, she began her drive in earnest. Schroeder encouraged members of DACOWITS to lobby their representatives and senators while she tried to round up votes in the House. She pointed out that arguing about whether women could serve in combat was a moot point. Women had been in very dangerous situations during Desert Storm, situations that most would have labeled "combat." Besides, there were no safe places in war anymore. Modern missiles could strike anyone anywhere, on or off the battlefield. Removing the official restrictions not only would be more honest, she argued, but it also could open up new opportunities for women in the military.

At the same time, there were many women who did not want the combat exclusion eliminated, including women returning from the war. It was true, they conceded, that Scud missiles could kill men and women anywhere, but there were still some positions that were more dangerous than others, and in their opinion, positions that should be off-limits to females.

TYRANNY, TERRORISM, AND THE TWIN TOWERS

CHAPTER THREE

" Does God have enough hands? "

> • Five-year-old Molly Vandevender's question
> upon being told by her mother that
> God had pulled the victims, including
> her father, up to heaven from
> the destruction at Ground Zero.

*D*esert Storm might have been a military victory, but it was not a complete success. The war and the continuing presence of U.S. troops in the Persian Gulf region after the war were part of a chain of events that culminated in the ultimate terrorist act against the United States on September 11, 2001.

TROUBLE BREWING IN THE GULF REGION

Saddam Hussein and his regime managed to survive the defeat of the Iraqi Army in the first Persian Gulf War. Because Hussein continued to be a threat, the U.S. military did not leave the Gulf region entirely after the cease-fire order that ended Operation Desert Storm. Occasionally, Iraqi aircraft defied the no-fly zone that banned the Iraqi Air Force from flying across the northern third of the country. In December 1992 and January 1993, coalition aircraft shot down Iraqi fighter jets flying through the zone.

In September and October of 1994, Hussein again decided to test his limits. He sent two armored divisions to the Iraq-Kuwait border. The United States responded by deploying 36,000 troops to Kuwait. Iraq retreated. U.S. and coalition aircraft continued to patrol the northern and southern thirds of Iraq. The aircraft flew from bases located in Turkey and the other Gulf states.

The continuing presence of Americans in the area angered many Arabs. These fundamentalists saw American soldiers as infidels defiling sacred ground. One of these Arabs was a man named Osama bin Laden. He blamed the United States for debasing Saudi Arabia with its "corrupting Western influences."[1] He vowed to lead a *jihad*, or "holy war," against the United States.

TERROR FROM THE SKIES

The cloudless, blue sky on the morning of September 11, 2001, held the promise of a beautiful late-summer day. It gave no indication of the horror that would soon be unleashed.

By 8 A.M. at the World Trade Center in New York City, thousands of people were starting their workday. In Washington, D.C., civilian and military personnel went about their early morning duties. At Newark International Airport in New Jersey, families excitedly boarded aircraft as they began their vacations, while businesspeople stowed their briefcases on their way to routine business trips.

At 8:48 A.M., American Airlines Flight 11 veered off its course from Boston to California and crashed into the North Tower of the World Trade Center. Stunned spectators assumed that a horrible accident had taken place. Few thought that the plane had intentionally crashed into the skyscraper. That belief ended when United Airlines Flight 175 crashed into the South Tower at 9:03 A.M. As television stations showed images of smoke and fire pouring from a gaping hole in the side of the North Tower, a stunned country realized that it was under attack.

Within thirty minutes, the Federal Aviation Administration (FAA) had closed down all airports in the country. Yet some planes were still in flight. Who was at the controls of these aircraft? At about 9:40 A.M., American Airlines Flight 77 crashed into the Pentagon, outside of Washington, D.C., killing everyone on board and more than one hundred Defense Department employees.

Back in New York City, police officers and firefighters rushed into the burning Twin Towers, trying to evacuate the thousands of employees who worked there. At approximately 10:00 A.M., less than an hour after the second tower had been struck by a plane, a loud rumbling noise was heard. The sky darkened as smoke and ash billowed out in a furious cloud down surrounding streets. Within seconds, the 110 floors of the South Tower collapsed into rubble—trapping and killing those who were attempting to exit the building. When the fully fueled plane had penetrated the structure, it had exploded in a fireball that was hot enough to melt the metal center supports of the skyscraper, resulting in the building's collapse. At 10:28 A.M., the horror was repeated as the North Tower fell.

As the smoke began to clear, a voice could be heard wailing: "Where did it go? Oh Lord, where did it go?"[2] In less than two hours, nearly 3,000 people—including hundreds of firefighters and police officers who had bravely entered the burning buildings to rescue the employees—had been killed in the collapse of the Twin Towers. A shaken John Maloney, who escaped from his office in the trade center, commented on the destruction: "I don't know what the gates of hell look like, but it's got to look like this. I'm a combat veteran, Vietnam, and I never saw anything like this."[3]

FAA officials attempted to make contact with all airborne craft. At 10 A.M., United Airlines Flight 93 crashed into a field outside of Shanksville, Pennsylvania, killing all passengers and the three terrorists. Because some of the passengers had made cell phone calls to or received calls from loved ones on the ground, they knew about the attacks on New York and Washington. They also knew that their plane would be used as a weapon. At 35,000 feet (10,668 m) above the ground, they vowed to stop the terrorists from taking more lives, even if they couldn't save their own.[4] When passenger Todd Beamer said, "Okay, let's roll!," a group of passengers used a food cart to storm the cockpit, where the terrorists had taken over the controls after killing the pilot and copilot. No one knows what happened next, but most Americans believe that these passengers acted heroically.[5]

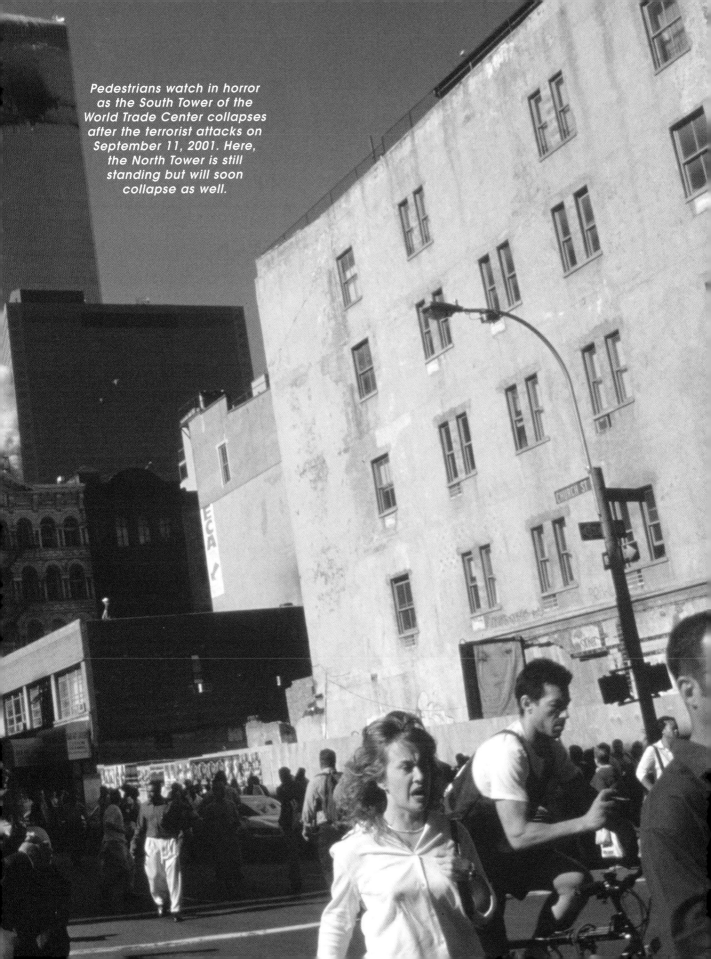

Pedestrians watch in horror as the South Tower of the World Trade Center collapses after the terrorist attacks on September 11, 2001. Here, the North Tower is still standing but will soon collapse as well.

In the days that followed the attacks on the Twin Towers, thousands of volunteers worked around the clock sifting through the debris of the destroyed buildings looking for survivors. Many of the workers at the 16-acre (6.5-hectare) scene, which was termed Ground Zero, were firefighters searching for their fallen comrades. When it became clear that there would be few if any survivors, the goal changed to recovering bodies for identification and proper burial.

Ground Zero came to be viewed as hallowed ground because it was the burial site of so many people. In the early hours after the attack, when New York City mayor Rudolph Giuliani was asked how many people might have died in the collapse of the towers, he replied, "It will be more than we can bear." He was right.

A NETWORK OF TERROR

The attacks were a terrifying dose of reality for many Americans, who quickly discovered a network of enemies they never knew they had. Americans learned of a deadly terrorist network called al Qaeda, whose members viewed the United States as an evil empire and thought their religious duty was to destroy it. The terrorists did not have an army powerful enough to face the U.S. military in direct combat, but they could stage individual attacks on U.S. targets. Often these were suicide attacks in which the terrorist was killed along with the victims. These men believed that their actions would bring them great rewards in the afterlife.

Al Qaeda is commanded by spiritual and military leader Osama bin Muhammad bin Laden. He is a mysterious and paradoxical leader. Although he was born to a wealthy family in Saudi Arabia in 1957—and inherited millions of dollars—he was content to live in the dusty caves of Afghanistan where he was given political haven. He is an outcast from his country, his family, and his religion, yet he is admired by millions of people in the Arab world for his holy war against the United States.

Bin Laden is an adherent of a radical and violent brand of Islam that most Muslims do not support. Bin Laden has worked with other terrorist leaders to form a worldwide terrorist network. He accuses the United States of being the source of every crisis and problem that afflicts the Muslim world.

Bin Laden was not a religious zealot in his youth. Like many other young affluent Arab men in the 1970s, he escaped the strict Muslim lifestyle to experience the flashy nightlife of Beirut, Lebanon. He gained a reputation as a drinker and a womanizer.[6] A personal transformation began in 1973, when he rebuilt two holy mosques. He began to study Islamic literature. He became troubled by the clash between Muslim values and the free-living ways of the Western world.

The strife between the Muslim world and Western civilization had begun to grow in the mid-1970s when the money earned from the sale of oil allowed many Saudis to purchase Western luxuries, such as televisions and Western-style clothing. Many Arabs saw American materialism as a threat to Islamic society, which is bound by strict codes of behavior. Some, like bin Laden, were prepared to use violence and terrorism to stop Western influences.

In 1979 the Muslim world was outraged when the Soviet Union invaded Afghanistan. An Islamic militant movement began to force the Communist invaders off Muslim land. Bin Laden used his own money to set up camps to train Arabs from the Persian Gulf states to join the Afghan resistance. By the mid-1980s, bin Laden was calling for an Afghan jihad—for Arabs everywhere to join the battle in Afghanistan. The ultimate goal of jihad is to establish the rule of Allah, the god of Islam, on Earth.

Throughout the 1980s, the royal family of Saudi Arabia supported bin Laden's efforts to purge influences that corrupted Islam. However, a rift occurred when the royal family allowed the United States to maintain a presence in the country after the Gulf War in 1991. This action was unacceptable to bin Laden.

War on Terror

In the wake of the attacks on 9/11, President George W. Bush, son of former president George H. W. Bush, vowed to wage a "War on Terror"—to destroy

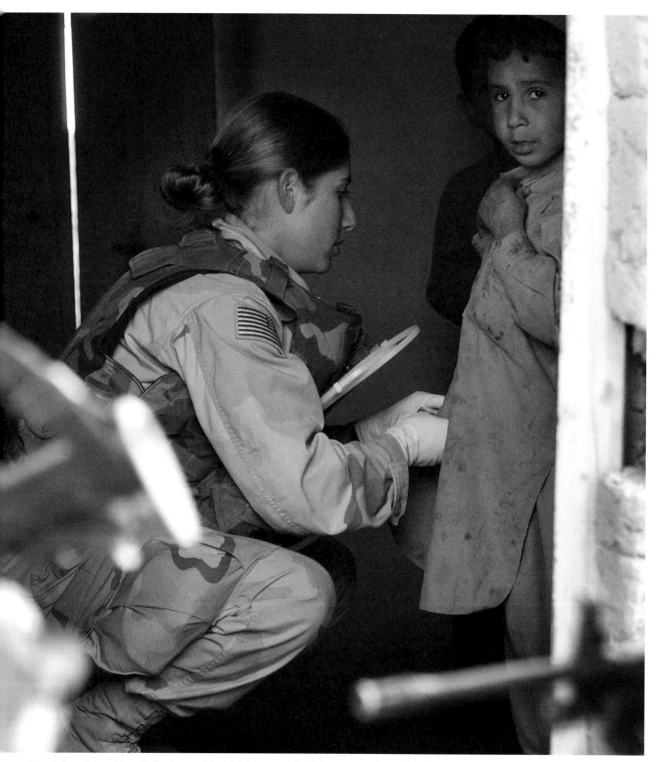

A soldier from the U.S. Army 82nd Airborne Division searches the home, as well as the children, of an Afghan family in November 2002 during Operation Alamo Sweep. The mission was intended to search villages in southeast Afghanistan for weapons and capture suspected al Qaeda or Taliban members.

the al Qaeda terrorist network. The president offered a multimillion-dollar reward for information leading to the capture of Osama bin Laden—either dead or alive. Currently one of the FBI's ten most-wanted fugitives, the reward for bin Laden's capture is $50 million.

To flush out bin Laden and the al Qaeda network, the United States sent soldiers to Afghanistan, where the terrorists had set up a base of operations. Weakened after years of battle with the Soviet Union, Afghanistan had been taken over by a repressive fundamentalist religious group called the Taliban. The Taliban allowed the terrorists to set up training camps in the country. Life was especially harsh for women under Taliban rule, because they were forbidden to attend school or have jobs. They were also forced to wear a garment called a *burka* that covered them from head to toe.

On October 7, 2001, U.S. forces bombed the Afghan city of Kandahar. The ensuing war in Afghanistan was not against the Afghan people, but to drive the Taliban and al Qaeda out of their stronghold in the mountains of the eastern part of the country. Because the terrorists could hide in Afghanistan's extensive network of caves, the U.S. military used a "scorched earth" tactic of dropping massive bombs, such as the 15,000-pound (6,804 kg) daisy cutter bombs that can obliterate an area hundreds of yards in diameter. After five months of rugged fighting in Afghanistan, U.S. troops had captured many al Qaeda terrorists, but bin Laden was not among them.[7]

On March 5, 2002, U.S. forces began a large ground offensive campaign called Operation Anaconda. It was an attempt to destroy all of the al Qaeda and Taliban fighters hiding in the mountains near the city of Kabul. With 2,000 U.S. soldiers, 500 Canadian soldiers, and hundreds of Afghan fighters, it was the largest ground operation in the conflict. By month's end, the Taliban and al Qaeda were finally routed from Afghanistan. However, bin Laden had once again escaped. His whereabouts remain unknown.[8]

Of the 5,200 U.S. soldiers in Afghanistan by March 2002, women composed 6 percent. In the Afghan conflict, American military women worked as military police, flew refueling and fighter planes, and served on warships. Soon, U.S. military women would face another war with an old enemy in the Middle East.

OPERATION IRAQI FREEDOM

CHAPTER FOUR

> "The qualities that are most important in all military jobs—things like integrity, moral courage, and determination— have nothing to do with gender."
> • **Major Rhonda Cornum**

Of the more than 250,000 soldiers sent to the Middle East as part of Operation Iraqi Freedom, one out of every seven was a woman. The second Persian Gulf War saw the largest deployment of women to a combat theater in U.S. history.

Currently, women make up almost 14 percent of the all-volunteer U.S. armed forces—a third more than at the time of the first Gulf War. The Air Force has the largest number of women soldiers with 20 percent, while the Army has 15 percent, the Navy 14 percent, and the Marines 6 percent. More than 40,000 women served in the war in 1991, and their excellent performance opened up new roles for women in the military.[1] In 1994, the risk rule, which had banned women from serving in units "at risk" for contact with the enemy or capture, was lifted.

Although women were allowed to serve in combat roles by the second Gulf War, they were still barred from units whose primary assignment was direct ground combat. This ban prevented them from serving in the infantry, in the armored and Special Forces units, and on submarine missions. However, women piloted fighter jets and helicopters, dropped bombs, launched Tomahawk missiles, returned fire if ambushed, and served as military police.[2] A woman soldier could fly a bomber, but she could not be one of the paratroopers who jumped out of the plane.[3]

The debate over whether or not women should be allowed to engage in ground combat draws strong views on both sides of the issue. Some people, like Elaine Donnelly, president of the Center for Military Readiness, believe that ground-combat soldiers must be fit and strong—and that men are naturally stronger than women because of their larger size and greater upper-body strength. Gender-normed training in the military measures equal effort instead of actual results, explained Donnelly. Because gender-norming doesn't exist on the battlefield, she claims that a female combat soldier's lack of strength could endanger her unit during warfare.[4]

Other people believe that women can hold their own on the battlefield because they go through the same training as men. Jacqueline Thompson was angered after making it through the grueling training to be a U.S. Marine only to be left behind at a desk job when her battalion was shipped off to war in Iraq. "We go through the same boot camp, so why shouldn't I be able to go over and fight?" Thompson asked in frustration.[5] Already, Canada, South Africa, and some Scandinavian countries allow women to fight in ground-combat missions.[6]

People opposed to sending women soldiers to the front lines claim that Americans are not prepared for females to be killed or captured. However, the events of the first Gulf War showed that the front lines have blurred in modern warfare. When an enemy fires long-range missiles, soldiers in the rear lines are in danger, too. Often, enemy fire is aimed at strategic targets such as supply areas and communication centers where women soldiers are frequently stationed.[7]

Build-Up to War

After the terrorist attacks on 9/11, the U.S. government began to worry even more that terrorists might get their hands on weapons of mass destruction, such as chemical or biological weapons. The government was especially concerned that Saddam Hussein would supply these weapons to terrorists who wanted to attack the United States.

From 1990 to 2002, Hussein repeatedly violated a total of seventeen UN Security Council resolutions (UNSCRs). These resolutions had been created to ensure that Iraq did not pose a threat to international peace and security. The final resolution, USNSCR 1441, was passed on November 8, 2002. It called for Iraq to reveal its weapons of mass destruction so that the country could be disarmed. That same month, UN weapons inspectors went to Iraq in to look for hidden stashes of weapons. Hussein's regime denied having any arsenals of chemical or nuclear weapons. By December 2002, the UN inspectors had yet to uncover any nuclear, chemical, or biological agents. However, they stated that Iraq was not cooperating fully. The inspectors believed that Iraqis moved evidence from some sites to private residences before the inspection visits.

In his State of the Union Address on January 28, 2003, President George W. Bush made his case to the American people for going to war with Iraq. In his speech, he claimed that Hussein was a danger to American security because he possessed weapons of mass destruction. Based on information gathered by British intelligence sources, the president stated that Iraq had purchased large quantities of uranium from Nigeria in Africa. These actions would signal that Iraq might already have a nuclear weapon capability. Based on this threat, the president urged that the United States wage a preemptive war against this threat.

In February, Secretary of State Colin Powell addressed the UN Security Council to convince members of the threat posed by Iraq. Brandishing a small vial of anthrax in his hand, he spoke of the dangers posed by even a tiny amount of a biological weapon. At that time, many UN members still were not convinced of the need for military action against Iraq.

Despite strong opposition to war from counties like France and Germany, the United States decided to stop working with the UN to find a diplomatic solution to the crisis with Iraq. In March, President Bush met with Prime Minister Tony Blair of Great Britain and President José Maria Aznar of Spain to discuss war plans. France's lack of support for military action in Iraq set off anti-French sentiment in the United States. Some Americans went so far as to rename french fries as "freedom fries." However, not all Americans supported a military solution to the Iraq situation, and they staged antiwar demonstrations.

On March 17, 2003, President George W. Bush issued an ultimatum to Saddam Hussein. He gave the Iraqi leader forty-eight hours to leave the country. If not, the coalition forces would lead a shock-and-awe attack against Iraq—that is, a massive and overwhelming strike to cripple Iraq's infrastructure. Bush's goal for declaring war with Iraq was twofold: to locate and destroy weapons of mass destruction and to remove Hussein from power so that a more democratic government could take the dictator's place.

By March 19, 2003, Bush's forty-eight-hour ultimatum had expired. Hussein rejected Bush's offer of lifetime exile, perhaps because he believed that the Arab world would unite behind him. At 10:15 P.M., President Bush addressed the United States to announce the start of Operation Iraqi Freedom. Just as his father did thirteen years earlier, this president would be sending women soldiers into conflict in the Middle East.

SHOCK AND AWE

The U.S. military began Operation Iraqi Freedom by launching a massive air strike against Iraqi targets. In the first round of air attacks, more than forty satellite-guided Tomahawk Cruise Missiles were fired from U.S. warships in the Red Sea and Persian Gulf. Because the army leadership suspected that Hussein might be hiding in an underground bunker, two F-17s dropped two 2,000-pound (907-kg) bombs on the suspected site. In what would become a pattern throughout the war, Hussein appeared to have escaped.

The ground war began on March 20 after the air strikes had softened Iraqi defenses. Because Turkey refused to allow the United States to invade Iraq from their country, the ground assault had to come from the south. The coalition forces planned a three-pronged attack that would set out from Kuwait.

In the first prong of the attack, British troops surrounded the city of Basra and seized Umm Qasr in southeastern Iraq. Coalition forces needed to gain control of Umm Qasr because it was the only city in Iraq with a seaport large enough to handle the shipments of humanitarian aid that would soon arrive. In another part of the attack, U.S. Marines moved up through Nasiriyah, past Al Kut, and into eastern Baghdad.

In the final thrust of the attack, the 3rd Infantry Division—the main part of the assault—headed north. The troops moved west of the Euphrates River as they pushed across the open desert. In total, the troops traveled across 350 miles (563 km) of arid, inhospitable desert. North of the city of Karbala, the infantry crossed the river as the troops headed toward Baghdad, the capital.[8]

Coalition troops faced stiff resistance as they headed north toward Baghdad. In Nasiriyah, the Marines fought to control two bridges that were needed by the troops to move north toward the capital. To capture these bridges, the Marines had to fight Iraqis who shot at them from nearby buildings. In the midst of this fighting to secure the route through Nasiriyah, a six-vehicle supply convoy became lost. The fifteen soldiers of the 507th Maintenance Unit were either killed or taken captive. One of the POWs was single mother Shoshana Johnson.

MOTHERS AT WAR

Shoshana Johnson was not the only mother to leave a child behind as she headed off to war. Lori Piestewa left behind two preschoolers. Nearly two thirds of women soldiers leave behind children when they are deployed to a battle zone.[9]

According to Kathleen Harris of the National Association of Black Military Women, many women join the armed services to "make a better home for their children. When they leave the service, they're often snapped up by civilian firms

Women were not only active during the war as soldiers. Some were busy on the home front opposing President Bush's decision to wage war against Saddam Hussein.

David Klemisch sits with his children while they hold teddy bears that play recorded messages from their mother who is at war in Iraq.

because they have knowledge and discipline."[10] Minorities are well represented in the Army. Forty-six percent of female enlistees are African American, whereas they represent only 14 percent of the general population of women aged eighteen to forty-four.

Many mothers in the armed forces have mixed feelings about leaving their children behind. They are proud to serve and protect their country, yet they miss sharing birthdays, first steps, and other milestones with their children. To cope, some mothers record their children's favorite stories so their children will remember the sound of their mother's voice. Other mothers put up maps of the Middle East in their children's bedrooms so that they will know where their mother is.

A soldier with a U.S. Army Infantry Division in Texas says good-bye to her daughter before deploying to Iraq in March 2003.

Because 41 percent of women soldiers have husbands who are also in uniform, the armed forces are becoming a family affair. When Lieutenant Colonel Laura Richardson, thirty-nine, and her husband, Lieutenant Colonel Jim Richardson, forty-two, headed off to Kuwait, they made history as the first married battalion commanders ever to fly into battle together. As commander of the 5th Battalion of the 101st Aviation Brigade, Laura Richardson led the Black Hawk helicopters that carried troops to the front lines of battle. She was one of only 112 women soldiers assigned to pilot a Black Hawk in the war, as compared with 2,230 men.[11]

Her husband led the Apache helicopters of the 3rd Battalion, which provided the firepower to protect these troops. When the Richardsons left for Kuwait, they had to leave behind their fourteen-year-old daughter, Lauren. Even though Laura Richardson was about to face the dangers of war, she stated: "The hardest thing about any deployment to the Gulf will be leaving [Lauren]."[12]

Road to Baghdad

The United States initially thought that Iraqi citizens would rise up against Hussein's regime once coalition forces began their invasion from the south. However, the expected uprising never occurred. The coalition forces were surprised by the resistance they faced from Iraqi troops. Perhaps some Iraqis were mistrustful because the United States did not support an Iraqi revolt after the first Persian Gulf War. Hussein was able to remain in power, which led to the torture and killing of thousands of Iraqis who had opposed him.

Coalition forces believed that the paramilitary group called the Fedayeen was responsible for most of the fierce resistance troops faced as they pushed north toward Baghdad. Led by Hussein's son Uday, these guerrilla-style fighters were loyal to Saddam Hussein and fanatically opposed to the presence of U.S. troops in Iraq. Fedayeen soldiers often drove sport utility vehicles or other civilian cars, making them more difficult to detect. Their preferred weapons were mortars (a type of cannon), rocket-propelled grenades, and machine guns.

Two U.S. Army soldiers—Private Miranda Nichols, eighteen, from Georgia, and Private First Class Leysha Williamson, twenty-seven, from Texas—keep watch from a foxhole during a defensive alert of the 3rd Infantry Division south of Baghdad.

U.S. troops were also confronted with deadly suicide bombings. The first suicide attack occurred on March 29, 2003. A taxi drove up to an army checkpoint near the city of Najaf. The driver waved to the soldiers for help. When the soldiers approached the taxi, the driver detonated a bomb, killing himself and four U.S. soldiers. In other attacks, Iraqi soldiers waved white flags in a gesture of surrender, only to open fire once they were close to the unsuspecting U.S. troops.

In addition to guerrilla attacks, the progress of the ground troops was also slowed by the weather. Blinding sandstorms made it difficult for soldiers to breathe, let alone see for any great distance in front of them. The sand also clogged vehicle engines and jammed weapons.

As the ground forces advanced toward Baghdad, coalition aircraft continued to blast Republican Guard units located around Baghdad. (Numbering about 80,000, these combat troops were Hussein's most loyal soldiers.) In the first Gulf War, women were not allowed to fly combat aircraft. In the second Gulf War, Air Force Captain Christina Hooper, twenty-seven, was the only woman to pilot an F-16 over Iraq. Her mission was to drop satellite-guided "smart" bombs. The precision of these bombs in hitting their targets is said to help minimize civilian casualties. Her closest call in combat happened one night when her plane was hit by lightning. Hooper recalled: "I could see sparks in front of my jet, and I wondered if I should stay in hostile territory or go home. I wanted the trip to be worthwhile, so I stayed and dropped my bombs."[13]

Hooper was not the only American woman to fly over the Iraqi skies. Another twenty women were trained to fly the Army's Longbow Apache helicopters. These models are considered to be the world's most technologically advanced helicopters. The Longbow can detect targets and protect troops on the ground. Unlike women soldiers in the first Gulf War, Captain Jennifer Johnson, twenty-seven, had the opportunity to fly one in this war. She explained, "I like to fly in the front seat, where I can control the battle."[14]

THE FALL OF BAGHDAD

In their march toward the capital, coalition forces discovered that hospitals and schools were being used by the Iraqi military to store weapons and ammunition. As the troops moved close to Baghdad, there were fears over chemical and biological weapons. Although gas masks and chemical protection suits were discovered, they found no caches of weapons. The soldiers also dreaded street-by-street urban fighting, because their high-tech weapons wouldn't give them an edge. The U.S. military also worried about the safety of Baghdad's five million civilians.

At daybreak on April 5, U.S. tanks rolled into Baghdad. U.S. troops had seized Saddam International Airport the previous day. The troops received a mixed welcome. While many residents greeted the Americans warmly, other Iraqis continued to fire their weapons.

As U.S. troops took over the city, they raided the opulent palaces built by Hussein and his sons. In a country where many people lacked food and clothing, the dictator enjoyed a lavish lifestyle. The plumbing in one of his palaces

After taking over Baghdad, the U.S. Marines camp out inside one of Hussein's opulent palaces in April 2003.

was plated with gold. And everywhere, there were pictures of the dictator striking heroic poses. In addition to the many portraits, Hussein also had statues of himself built across the country. These statues were a testament to his enormous ego.

On April 9, U.S. Marines helped Iraqi citizens topple a statue of the dictator in Baghdad Square. Before the statue fell, one enthusiastic marine scaled the monument to place an American flag over Hussein's face. Quickly realizing that this act sent the wrong message—that the United States was taking over the country—the flag was immediately replaced by the Iraqi flag. After the statue was felled, jubilant Iraqis dragged its head throughout the streets. The destruction of the statue was a visual sign that Hussein's regime had fallen.

Fortunately, the fears of the U.S. military over urban combat, chemical weapons, and civilians trapped by the war did not materialize. However, other problems emerged in the days that followed the capture of Baghdad. After years of repression, Iraqi citizens went on a looting rampage. Television news reports showed hundreds of Iraqis carrying chairs and computers out of buildings. Unfortunately, the looters also stole badly needed medical supplies from hospitals. On April 12, looters broke into Iraq's national museum, stealing seven thousand years' worth of priceless artifacts. Without a police force to keep order, there was anarchy on the streets.

In the days that followed the fall of Baghdad, many of the once jubilant crowds began to display hostility toward U.S. troops. Some Iraqis who had greeted the troops with cheers and hugs only days earlier, now demanded their removal. Cheers of "liberation" turned into taunts of American "occupation."[15]

Yet there was still more work to be done. The coalition forces needed to capture cities in northern Iraq. With the help of Kurdish forces in the north, the cities of Mosul and Dohuk fell without much of a fight. From there U.S. troops headed to Hussein's hometown of Tikrit, which quickly fell as well.

On May 1, three weeks after the fall of Baghdad, President Bush declared an end to major combat in Iraq. The process of nation-building needed to begin.

Facing Page: Iraqi civilians use a rope to try to bring down the enormous statue of Saddam Hussein in downtown Baghdad.

IRAQ'S MOST-WANTED CHARACTERS

In addition to Saddam Hussein and his two sons, Uday and Qusay, coalition forces were in search of dozens of other key figures in Iraq's government and military. To help soldiers identify these people, the Pentagon createed a deck of playing cards of the fifty-five Iraqis most wanted by the U.S. government. On April 11, 2003, the U.S. military issued two hundred sets of playing cards to U.S. soldiers. Each card in the deck showed the face of one of Iraq's infamous regime leaders. Saddam, the number one target, had his face printed on the ace of spades.

On the five of hearts was Huda Salih Mahdi Ammash, the only female in the deck. Nicknamed Mrs. Anthrax by U.S. officials, the microbiologist was accused of overseeing research in Iraq's biological weapons program. One of the top women in Hussein's former regime, Ammash surrendered to coalition forces on May 9. By late 2004, forty-three of Iraq's most wanted had been either captured or killed.

HUDA SALIH MAHDI AMMASH
WMD Scientist/
Ba'th Party Regional
Command Member

SAVING LIVES DURING THE GULF WARS

CHAPTER FIVE

> " I'm looking forward to knowing
> I can make a difference. "
> • **Dianna McCoy, Reserve Medical Unit**

American women have not only served in the armed forces during each and every conflict, but they have also cared for America's wounded during these wars, even when doing so put them in danger. During the American Revolution, female volunteers bandaged soldiers' wounds in makeshift hospitals. They carried soup and blankets to captives afflicted with smallpox.

During the Civil War, women were allowed to serve both as volunteers and, for the first time in American military history, as combat nurses. In that conflict, it was not uncommon for a battle to result in one thousand or more casualties in a single day. The North and South were so poorly prepared to handle these injuries that both sides had to ask citizens to help treat injured soldiers in their homes. The volunteers did so well that government officials, desperately short of male nurses, eventually decided to take women into the medical corps. To make sure that there would be no scandalous behavior between nurses and patients, women who applied for work had to be plain in appearance and considerably older than the soldiers they would treat. These women also had to forego anything that might improve their appearance, such as dresses or even ribbons in their hair.

The nurses proved beyond any doubt during the Civil War that they could deal with the most shocking wounds, even assisting during amputations while under enemy fire. So when America declared war on Spain in 1898, few objected to sending female nurses, plain or pretty, with the medical corps. But the government struggled mightily to find enough qualified nurses on short notice.

To avoid a nursing shortage in the future, the Army established the Army Nurse Corps in 1901. The Navy established a similar corps in 1908. From then on, the armed services would have a professional supply of nurses that it could rely on at all times. However, even though female physicians served in both World Wars I and II, neither the Army nor the Navy would accept women doctors as a permanent part of the medical corps until late in the twentieth century.

MEDICS OF DESERT STORM

Each war in U.S. history has presented special challenges for women. Operation Desert Storm was no exception. Like the armed services and their extensive reserve system, the Army and Navy medical corps were also dependent on thousands of reservists, including female nurses, doctors, and surgeons. These participants, who were scattered all over the country, had never worked together. As a result, their first challenge was to form close-knit teams as quickly as possible. To do this, medical personnel who were called to the Persian Gulf region met first at various military bases throughout the United States. At the bases, classes were held to create these teams and to prepare participants for life in the desert—another unique challenge—before heading to Saudi Arabia.

Once medical personnel arrived in the Middle East, most Army staff members and reservists were assigned to one of four kinds of makeshift "hospitals." These were either huge tents surrounded by sandbags or temporary buildings complete with air-conditioning that were assembled from prefabricated materi-

Off-duty nurses take a break outside the tents of Fleet Hospital 15, which was established for Desert Storm.

als in only a few days. Some medics joined battalion aid stations, which were located near the front lines when the ground war began. Injured soldiers were brought here first for help and evaluation of their wounds. Others reported to mobile Army surgical hospitals, which operated approximately 50 miles (80 km) behind the front, following the troops as they advanced.

A third group of medics was assigned to combat-support hospitals, which remained at least 100 miles (160 km) behind the lines. These hospitals accepted local citizens who needed care as well as prisoners of war who needed medical attention. And finally, a fourth group staffed evacuation hospitals, which were located near airfields. Wounded soldiers who needed special medical care would be held here until they could be transported to medical facilities in Europe.

Once established in their hospitals, medical teams continued their classes, deciding how best to operate in emergency situations, including how to treat fatally wounded soldiers. Elizabeth Kassner, a nurse assigned to a combat-support hospital, explained in a letter to her parents that there was disagreement over whether the fatally injured should be told how serious their condition was: "One doctor was saying he'll be honest and up front with these people and tell them we don't have the resources to save them. I told him I could not and would not do that. That deep in my heart and soul, I will always pray for a miracle."[1]

CLARA L. ADAMS-ENDER
BRIGADIER GENERAL ARMY NURSING CORPS

Brigadier General Clara L. Adams-Ender was head of the Army Nursing Corps during Desert Storm. She was well-qualified for this demanding position. After graduating from high school at sixteen, Adams-Ender, who was one of ten children, earned a degree in nursing from North Carolina Agricultural and Technical State University. She joined the Army Nursing Corps in 1961. After serving all over the world, she attended the U.S. Army Command and Staff College in Fort Leavenworth, Kansas, where she became the first woman to earn the degree Master of Military Art and Science. In 1982 she became the first black nursing corps officer to graduate from the U.S. Army War College.

In 1986, Adams-Ender became the chief of nursing at Walter Reed Army Medical Center, the largest armed services health-care facility in the United States. One year later, she became the eighteenth chief of the Army Nursing Corps, a position she held until August 1991.

In addition to facing the typical horrors of war, medical personnel steeled themselves for chemical and biological attacks, which Saddam Hussein had repeatedly threatened to launch during Operation Desert Storm. No one other than Hussein had used poison gas since World War I, so few—if any—doctors or nurses had real-life experiences with chemical weapons. During drills, men and women practiced donning gas masks and protective suits and gloves as quickly as possible, and then they went over the latest techniques for decontaminating victims. Even though they drilled repeatedly, there was still great apprehension. As one official said, "Everyone knows what to do and knows how to do it, but they have never done it for real."[2]

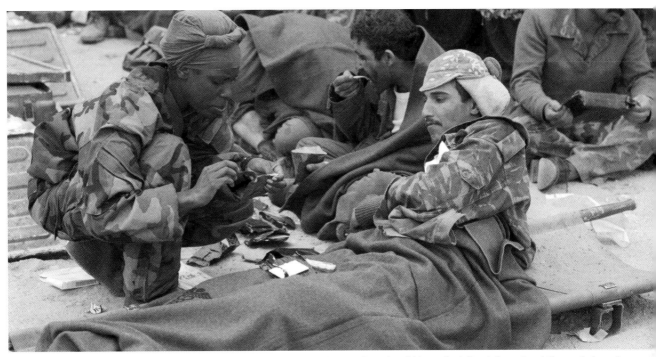

A female soldier of the 5th MASH FST (Mobile Army Surgical Hospital Fast Surgical Team) tends to the wounds of American and Iraqi soldiers somewhere on the Gulf War front.

Although Saddam Hussein bragged about the brutal war he would wage, once coalition troops marched into Iraq and then Kuwait, his troops proved anything but fierce. In fact, most Iraqi soldiers couldn't surrender fast enough when facing overwhelming force. Coalition troops rounded up more than 80,000 prisoners of war in less than one hundred hours. Medical teams had no way of knowing this would happen, though, and they were prepared for the worst.

Because Iraq proved to be a far weaker enemy than anticipated, the number of combat casualties never reached the early predictions of 10,000 to 20,000 victims. This didn't mean that medical corps personnel had little opportunity to put their expertise to work, however. American troops, almost a half million strong, suffered from all kinds of diseases in the desert: reactions to the many immunizations they had received before being sent to the region, dehydration, and accidental injuries. One hospital admitted more than one thousand patients and performed more than one hundred operations during the short war. Another treated more than eight thousand outpatients.

Among the most difficult patients to treat were prisoners of war. Nurse Elizabeth Kassner described her experiences:

We received 140 plus Iraqi [prisoners of war] in thirty-six hours. These guys are sick. They have gunshot wounds, shrapnel wounds, they've been wandering the desert for days. . . . There is no history. We basically guess at what is truly wrong with them. The docs are so busy that I [am giving] pain meds, oxygen, and antibiotics. . . . And they of course don't speak English. We do a lot of charades trying to determine what hurts, did they fall, or something fall on them and so on. It is hard, and my emotional stability is shot.[3]

The Navy also provided medical care. The U.S.N.S. *Comfort*, a floating hospital that could house one thousand patients, was brought to the Persian Gulf. In addition, the Navy operated fleet hospitals that provided care near the front lines. One commander in the Navy Nurse Corps described working very hard, sometimes putting in twenty hours a day to care for patients in a fleet hospital.

In previous wars, female medical personnel usually remained behind the battle lines. During Desert Storm, at least one woman, Major Rhonda Cornum, an Army flight surgeon, went into enemy territory on a rescue mission. On February 27, a pilot who survived a crash 60 miles (97 km) behind the Iraqi border radioed for help. He had a broken leg, making it impossible for him to leave the site on his own, and Iraqi soldiers were not far away. A rescue team, which included Cornum, was immediately sent to find him, treat his injuries as much as possible on the scene, and bring him back to safety. After grabbing her medical gear, Cornum and a seven-man flight crew took off. Cornum described the experience:

We flew as fast as we could, over a bunch of our guys, moving east. A few minutes after we saw the last friendly convoy, we started taking small-arms and antiaircraft fire. Seconds later we got hit, then we crashed. After we tumbled and rolled, I found myself underneath at least part of the wreck. I wasn't thinking clearly enough to know why I couldn't use my arms. I used one foot to kind of push my way out from underneath this airplane. By the time I got out, the Iraqi soldiers were there.[4]

Cornum broke both arms during the incident. She and the two other surviving members of the crew were taken to Baghdad, where they were held as prisoners of war until March 6, when they were released. Although Captain Bill Andrews, whom Cornum's team had been sent to rescue, was initially thought to be missing in action, he was later found in Baghdad suffering from a broken leg.

Because of the difficult situations medical personnel faced during the first Gulf War, by the end of the conflict, more than a few nurses and doctors saw themselves in a different light. Nurse Elizabeth Kassner spoke for many when she said: "Desert Storm challenged me physically, professionally and emotionally. I became a stronger person. . . . [We] had to depend on each other and work together as a team to survive in that frightful, desolate situation."[5]

POW Major Rhonda Cornum was released to the International Committee of the Red Cross in Baghdad on March 6, 1991, after having sustained two broken arms. Generals Khalid Bin Sultan (left) and Norman Schwarzkopf were there to greet her.

OLD CONCERNS IN A NEW WAR

Soon after the first Persian Gulf War ended, many soldiers began to suffer from a variety of mysterious symptoms such as memory loss, insomnia, rashes, hair loss, weight loss, chronic fatigue, and an inability to concentrate. Doctors were initially baffled because the symptoms did not fit into a simple category. Eventually, these symptoms were grouped together under the diagnosis of Gulf War Syndrome.

Army doctor Colonel Paula K. Underwood was one of the first physicians to encounter a soldier exhibiting the unusual symptoms of Gulf War Syndrome. After returning from the war, the young soldier began to experience memory loss. It became so severe that he could no longer find his way home from work or remember how to make his morning coffee. From 1991 to 1993, Underwood treated seventy-two patients with unexplained illnesses who had served in the Persian Gulf War.

In 2003, based on her previous experience with Gulf War Syndrome, Underwood worked with other Army physicians to protect the health of soldiers sent to the second Gulf War. The Pentagon ordered health screenings for every one of the approximately 250,000 troops sent to fight in Operation Iraqi Freedom. Within thirty days of returning to the United States, each soldier was required to fill out a health questionnaire for review with a doctor. Soldiers were asked whether they had developed unusual symptoms while deployed, such as rashes or unrelenting coughs. They were also asked about any possible exposure they might have had to chemical or biological weapons, or even oil fires or pesticides. Finally, they were required to give a blood sample to be used for analysis in case symptoms developed later on.

This military-wide effort was intended to help avoid the delays and denials soldiers faced upon their return from the first Gulf War. "We're prepared this time, whereas in the first Gulf War we really weren't," Underwood explained. "We're doing it across the board and we're not waiting for them [ill soldiers] to come to us. When I stop and think about it, this is unprecedented in military medicine."[6]

THE FLOATING HOSPITAL USED AGAIN

In 2003, the U.S.N.S. *Comfort* returned to the Persian Gulf to treat the wounded of the second Gulf War. Once again, the ship was prepared to handle injuries from chemical attacks as well as other wartime injuries. Seven of the ship's 157 nurses, like Lieutenant Commander Mary Brantley, had sailed on the *Comfort* in Operation Desert Storm. Brantley said she never expected to be back on the *Comfort* for another war with Iraq.

Another war veteran on the *Comfort*, nurse anesthetist Captain Debra Yarema, had served with a busy Navy fleet hospital during Operation Desert Storm. Memories came flooding back as the *Comfort* began receiving its first patients. "My emotions were pretty upset when the war began and we started receiving casualties," she stated. She is still shaken by her memories of the first Gulf War: "Sirens would go off and we would have to wear our MOP (chemical) gear. There would be soldiers in body bags, people who shouldn't have been at war were having heart attacks. I'm glad I'm stationed on a ship further from the front lines this time."[7]

By the end of the first week of Operation Iraqi Freedom, the *Comfort* had received forty patients, including twenty with combat-related injuries. Many on board were surprised that the first casualty brought to the ship was not an American soldier but an Iraqi one. In addition to U.S. soldiers, the floating hospital treated coalition troops, Iraqi soldiers and civilians, and Iraqi freedom fighters. According to the ship's commander, Captain Chuck Blackenship, M.D., all individuals injured on the battlefield—whether friend or foe—must be given medical treatment.

Although only twenty-five years old, hospital medic Christina Colla felt well prepared to treat war casualties when the *Comfort* arrived in Gulf waters. Colla had formerly worked as an emergency medical technician (EMT) in New York City. As an EMT, she had responded to the site of the World Trade Center attacks on the morning of September 11, 2001. Colla had helped people to escape from the Twin Towers. "That experience gave me the background I need to work in this environment," she explained. "I had been thinking about joining the Navy, and September 11 gave it [her decision] more urgency."[8]

MEDICAL CENTER OF IRAQI FREEDOM

Military nurses and doctors in Kuwait and Iraq were also busy on land during Operation Iraqi Freedom. Dr. Maria O'Rourke was a staff surgeon at the 47th Combat Support Hospital. Constructed almost overnight in the Kuwaiti desert, the sprawling, 300-bed medical complex covers nearly 12

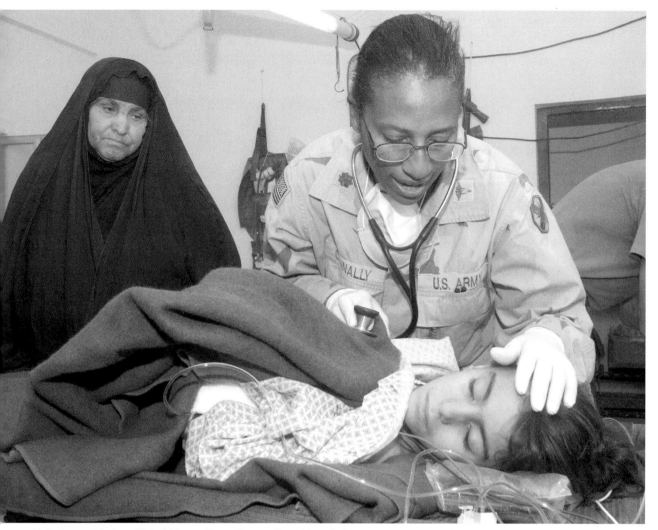

U.S. Army Major, Chief Nurse Tina Connally, attends to a seven-year-old Iraqi girl who was just operated on for shrapnel wounds while the girl's grandmother looks on. According to the doctors, she was injured by an Iraqi land-mine explosion near her home on the outskirts of Baghdad.

acres (4.9 hectares). The complex contains many of the facilities that can be found at large medical centers in the United States. In addition to four operating rooms, the center has radiology units and medical laboratories. The desert hospital is covered by air-conditioned tents that are pressurized to keep out dust from the desert.

On some days the medical complaints were minor, such as a soldier inhaling too much desert dust. Other times, the work at the hospital was grim. In one twelve-hour period in late March 2003, the hospital treated twenty-three soldiers who had been injured in six separate incidents, including firefights in Iraq.

The doctors worked quickly to treat soldiers whose injuries included gunshot wounds, open-skull wounds, amputations, and a mortar wound to the head. Incoming wounded were evaluated according to the triage system: Despite rank—or even which army the soldier was fighting for—the most critically injured went to the head of the line for treatment.

O'Rourke said that it was common for soldiers to downplay the severity of their injuries so that they could be sent back into battle. After a long stint treating injured soldiers, she paused to comment on their tenacity:

> *We even had a soldier tonight, all he kept saying was "Is this going to hold me back?" I tried to tell him, "Let's give it a few days." It's hard for them to face the fact that they are not going to go back and fight because they really want to be with their unit.*[9]

During peacetime, O'Rourke works in the emergency room of a hospital in Washington State. She says that she feels more of a personal connection with her patients at the Combat Support Hospital than with the ones back home. "It's different because you know that person could be you, or any other soldier that I know," she explained.[10]

RUGGED CONDITIONS AT MAKESHIFT HOSPITALS

While the combat hospital in Kuwait boasted facilities comparable to many U.S. medical centers, conditions at makeshift hospitals in Iraq were more rugged. Set up in the middle of an airfield near Nasiriyah, the 86th Combat Support Hospital had two operating rooms. It also had a film of dust that covered nearly every inch of the hospital. When the desert winds kicked up, doctors and patients alike quickly put on surgical masks to keep the dust out of their lungs.

Colonel Harry Warren, an orthopedic surgeon and the hospital's commanding officer, also served in Operation Desert Storm. In the first war, most of his patients were Iraqi prisoners of war who slowly trickled into the hospital.

Warren was stunned by the number of casualties coming into the hospital in the second Gulf War. Within forty-eight hours of his arrival at the hospital, two Marine helicopters had landed that were overloaded with thirty patients each. This group was quickly followed by two Black Hawk helicopters and an Army ambulance that brought dozens more patients. The hospital had been stocked with enough supplies to last for six days. Because of the heavy casualties, half the supplies were used up in a single day.

Despite the large number of U.S. soldiers sent to the hospital, most of the patients were Iraqi soldiers and civilians. Again, the rule of triage decided which patients received care first: The most severely injured were treated first—whether American, coalition, or Iraqi.

One of the hardest decisions faced by the hospital's staff was acknowledging that a critically injured three-year-old Iraqi girl was beyond medical help. The child had been shot when some men jumped out of the bus she was riding in and began a firefight with American soldiers. The girl's head wound showed severe damage to her skull and brain. Because she had no chance of survival, she was moved aside so that patients with less-critical injuries could be treated.

"I let my guard down on that one," said Sergeant Wendy Oehlman, a twen-ty-four-year-old nurse stationed at the hospital. "I stepped over for a moment to pray for her." As the nurse put her stethoscope to the little girl's chest, she heard the child's last gasp. "That just about finished me off," Oehlman said.[11]

The sadness felt by Oehlman and the rest of the staff over the little girl's death was somewhat appeased by the miraculous recovery of one Iraqi man. The patient had been brought to the hospital with a severe brain injury. A couple of days later, he was able to sit up and move about, although he still could not talk. Warren summed up the staff's feelings: "We thought there was almost no chance he would make it. It's things like that that make up for what we had to deal with."[12]

Many of the brave doctors and nurses stationed in Iraq would probably agree with twenty-two-year-old Ensign Adrian Harwood. A staff nurse aboard the U.S.N.S. *Comfort*, she commented during her tour of duty: "Even if you walk away from war physically unharmed, you don't walk away emotionally unchanged."[13]

REPORTING THE GULF WARS

CHAPTER SIX

> " If you want to be loved, don't
> go into our business. "
> • **Helen Thomas, journalist**

The media coverage in both Persian Gulf wars marked significant advancements in war reporting. In the first war, satellite technology allowed viewers around the world to watch the war in "real time" as events occurred. Never before had the public witnessed the beginning of military hostilities as they did with the first air strikes on January 17, 1991.

Although television viewers from around the world saw an unprecedented amount of live coverage of Operation Desert Storm, many journalists complained that the military restricted their access to information. These restrictions were lifted during the second war. For the first time in history, journalists were "embedded" with the troops in the field. As they accompanied the troops, they actually became part of the war they were covering. Some observers questioned whether the close connection of the journalists with the troops affected the reporters' objectivity. Reporters also faced the same dangers as the soldiers with whom they traveled.

REPORTING OPERATION DESERT STORM

Within hours after Saddam Hussein had invaded Kuwait in 1991, the American public eagerly sought information about events in the Persian Gulf region. This quest for information grew dramatically in the coming days and months as U.S. troops moved into the area. While modern technology could provide the tools that would make it possible for Americans to know almost instantly what was happening in the desert, the question of who would provide the information was hotly contested.

Although more than fifteen years had passed since the Vietnam War ended, some military leaders still resented the media and the coverage it had given to America's last major conflict. These leaders believed that journalists had portrayed it negatively and that their reports had turned the public against the war, making it impossible for the United States to win. Therefore, the armed services wanted to control what was said about Desert Shield and Desert Storm.

Also, because accounts on television could easily be intercepted or viewed by the enemy—Saddam Hussein was especially fond of Cable News Network (CNN) programs—leaders were loathe to turn journalists loose and let them say what they wanted when they wanted. U.S. newscasters might inadvertently reveal to the enemy more than the military wanted them to know.

So military leaders devised a special media program that would disclose a well-censored version of the war. Spokespersons from the armed forces and the state department gave regular briefings about events in the Gulf region. They showed video clips of the latest armaments in action and provided graphs to chart the progress of U.S. troops. Television networks could film the briefings, and journalists could question the speakers and then file their stories. This was best for everyone, the military said, especially journalists who had no business dodging bullets in the desert.

Many journalists thought that this was too much like the early reporting in Vietnam, when military sources supplied all the information—some of which

CARYLE MURPHY

JOURNALIST

While journalists were scrambling to get access to American troops as soon as Desert Shield began, a handful of reporters who happened to be in Kuwait when Iraq invaded tried their best to tell what was going on in the conquered nation. One of these reporters was Caryle Murphy, the Washington Post's bureau chief in Cairo, Egypt.

Despite the fact that Iraqi troops were rounding up foreigners, Murphy avoided detection for twenty-six days. From the seventh floor of the Safir International Hotel in Kuwait City and the streets of the capital, Murphy noted small but stiff pockets of resistance when the Iraqis tried to take the royal palace only two blocks away. She also reported massive destruction of buildings and symbols that represented Kuwait as the Iraqis tried to destroy the country's identity, and disappearing foodstuffs from stores as ordinary Kuwaitis tried to prepare themselves for a long occupation.

Murphy sent her first reports by telephone. When the Iraqis cut all lines of communication, she sent her reports with people who were planning to leave the country. Her byline and identity were kept secret to protect her until she, too, decided to leave Kuwait, making a daring dash across the desert in a car caravan into Saudi Arabia.

After arriving in Saudi Arabia, Murphy continued to cover the war. She often saw the events in a different light, in large part because she had lived in the Middle East for many years. Murphy's determination to be an eyewitness was duly noted. In late 1990, she received one of the International Women's Media Foundation's annual Courage in Journalism Awards.

was highly suspect. This time reporters wanted more direct access to troops in the battlefield. The American public was also hesitant to accept the military's version of events in the Middle East, so there was growing pressure to allow the press to report from the battlefield. This didn't mean that the public completely trusted the media, however. Some Americans, like some military leaders, blamed journalists for losing the war in Vietnam.

As in previous wars, a compromise was eventually worked out between the leaders of major news organizations and military officials. Journalists would be allowed to go to the Gulf region. On any given day, a limited number of these journalists could interview the soldiers and then share what they had seen and heard with other reporters. Most of the journalists who were left behind stayed in a hotel in Dhahran, Saudi Arabia, and were dubbed "hotel warriors." They based their articles on information gathered from the small group of journalists who had access to the action. This was known as the pool system.

Anyone could sign up for a pool position, but it might take months before a reporter's name rose to the top of the list, enabling him or her to go to the front. Pools were created for television, newspaper, magazine, and radio correspondents as well as for photographers. The representatives from the five pools were to be accompanied by government information officers, who would help the men and women in the field get their reports or film back to Dhahran.

More than one thousand reporters, including one hundred women, decided to go to the Middle East. One of the most influential members of the television pool was CNN, and one of its most famous reporters during the war was Christiane Amanpour. A graduate of the University of Rhode Island, Amanpour had witnessed many dramatic scenes before she covered Desert Storm. As a teenager, Amanpour had fled from Iran with her family in 1979 during the Iranian revolution.

Amanpour began to cover events in the Gulf region shortly after U.S. troops arrived. She often wore a gas mask and helmet when going into the field to talk to soldiers. Her live reports brought firsthand accounts into millions of homes, making the conflict seem very real to viewers. Although women had filmed reports during the Vietnam War, few provided the amount and depth of coverage that Amanpour did during Desert Shield and Desert Storm.

Even though what she was doing was dangerous, Amanpour refused to be deterred. When asked several years later why anyone would want to be a war correspondent, she replied, "Because the world will care once they see our stories . . . because if we the storytellers don't do this, then the bad guys will win."[1]

Although some journalists accepted the pool system without argument, others were not happy with this arrangement for at least three reasons. First, it denied them a chance to decide what to report. They were dependent upon the correspondents who were allowed in the field to choose the topic. For example, a writer for *Mirabella*, a women's magazine, brought back information about women's lives near the front that several news organizations considered worthless.

CNN correspondent Christiane Amanpour covers the U.S.-led peacekeeping operation in Mogadishu, Somalia, in 1992. From a tower she watches Somali civilians crowding around the U.S. Marines.

Second, the pool system made all the reporters dependent on those who witnessed the action. Were their facts correct? If not, the coverage would be flawed, and the writers whose byline accompanied the articles, which were sent to hometown newspapers, would be held responsible. And third, reporters believed that without direct access to soldiers at the front lines, they could not accurately describe the emotions and thoughts of the troops—an important part of being a war correspondent.

But the only other choices—going into the desert on their own, thereby risking arrest by U.S. military forces, or attaching themselves to a military unit and risking capture by the Iraqis—were not acceptable to most journalists. Few were prepared to rough it in the desert, and fewer generals would allow journalists to accompany their soldiers.

Determined to do so anyway, some women pointed to a long line of successful women war correspondents—especially Peggy Hull (World War I), Sonia Tomara and Helen Kirkpatrick (World War II), and Marguerite Higgins, who won a Pulitzer Prize in 1951 for her coverage of the Korean conflict—as proof that they should be given a chance to travel with the troops. At least two persuasive females, Martha Teichner and Molly Moore, were given the opportunity to travel with the troops during Desert Storm.

Martha Teichner, an experienced war correspondent for the Columbia Broadcasting System (CBS), had covered conflicts in El Salvador, Northern Ireland, and the Middle East. She spent nearly five weeks with her crew scouting out the possibility of traveling with the 1st Armored Division. When she was finally given permission to do so, she was told that she had to provide a vehicle and driver and supplies for her crew, all of which she managed to obtain. The film the crew shot was to be taken from the front lines to Dhahran by a courier.

When Teichner realized that the courier could not read a map correctly, she abandoned the idea of traveling with the troops. Teichner said: "I was worried that [the courier] would take the stuff and drive into a mine field. That would mean I would get him killed. I couldn't live with that."[2] Teichner returned to Dhahran, where she anchored daily reports based on information gathered by the television pool. "There was every incentive in this war to be a hotel warrior," she added.[3]

Molly Moore, the senior military correspondent for the *Washington Post*, was more successful. She received permission from the commanding general of the Marine forces in the war, Lieutenant General Walter E. Boomer, whom she had previously interviewed, to travel with Boomer's troops when they invaded Kuwait. While the U.S. Army attacked Hussein's men along the Iraqi-Kuwaiti border, Boomer's soldiers were to attack Hussein's men along the Kuwaiti–Saudi Arabian line, forcing Iraqi soldiers to fight all along Kuwait's boundaries in the sand.

As prepared as Molly Moore was for this war, she found the four days she traveled with the fighting forces, especially in the first hours, downright terrifying. She later wrote:

The night was so black I could see nothing but the two taillights of the
armored war wagon a few yards ahead, piercing the darkness like a pair
of sinister red eyes. Each time they seemed on the verge of disappearing,
the driver pressed the accelerator, fearful of losing our guide through the
dark. The radio next to me crackled with a running catalogue of the
dangers that lurked outside.
"Stay close. There's unexploded ordnance out there. Stay to the right!"
"Be careful on your left. Booby-trapped machine gun!"
We strained to hear the distorted radio voices. I barely breathed,
expecting our [jeep] to explode any minute as we inched along
the narrow lanes that had been cleared through the battlefield
carpet of unexploded American bombs and Iraqi-laid [land] mines.[4]

Later her fear of being killed by a land mine was replaced with the fear of
capture. She continued her narrative:

"Dismounted infantry on your right!" the radio voice shouted.
"We don't know whether they are good guys or bad guys!"
Another voice cut into the transmission: "More on my left! They have
their hands up. About a dozen."
"Watch out! Watch out!" screamed the first voice. "They have weapons
and are in a prone position behind the berms!"
. . . We're surrounded, I thought, gripping the Kevlar helmet in my lap.
I slipped it over my head and tightened the chin strap. I pulled my flak
jacket more snugly around my chest . . . [and] waited for the gunfire
to begin.[5]

Although Moore expected to be captured, the Iraqi soldiers that the Marines
encountered quickly surrendered. After this scene was repeated a number of
times, the soldiers and Moore began to fear a trick. Were these Iraqis luring the
Americans into a false sense of security far from their base of support, prepared
to surround them at any moment? These fears proved baseless, but at that time
deep in the desert in the middle of the night, they seemed possible, even likely.

EVERYONE IN THE POOL

The pool of approximately one hundred photographers was dominated by major newsmagazines and news services such as *Newsweek* and the Associated Press. Representatives from these organizations shot more than one thousand photos each day, from which twenty were chosen as the official pictures of the day. Because it was difficult to get a slot in the pool, and the government imposed very strict rules regarding what could be taken and even what type of film was to be used, many photographers refused to be part of the pool.

In some cases, whole organizations, such as Sygma, boycotted the system. Sygma's president, Eliane Laffont said: "The photographers were losing their freedom. When you are told what to do, where and how to do it, and what to do with your material after it is done, in essence you are working for the [government]. And the Sygma photographers did not want to do that."[6]

While some photographers headed into the desert on their own, Sygma photographers covered events that pool photographers didn't: the emotional departure of the American troops; their arrival in Saudi Arabia; how the troops lived and trained in the desert; and events on the home front.

Sygma photographer Nola Tully pictured the human costs of the war. She covered the funeral of Captain Manuel Rivera Jr., one of the first soldiers to die in the conflict. Tully chose to snap her camera's shutter at the exact moment the Marines presented a flag to Rivera's mother. "The soldier's mother was paralyzed with grief," Tully recalled later. "A group of Marines folded the flag from her son's coffin, and one turned, stood before her, and bowed to hand her the flag. His gesture was so simple. It said what could never be spoken."[7]

Although many journalists and photographers like Tully tried to share as much as they could about the war, many photos and stories never made it into print. The subjects were not only limited by the pool system, but the war progressed so quickly that battles in the morning were often ignored, replaced by reports of more recent—and sometimes more dramatic—clashes in the afternoon. In addition, once U.S. troops entered Kuwait, the public wanted to hear about peace and triumph, not fighting and sacrifice. As a result, more than one story was scrapped, making the history of the war incomplete. And as in all previous wars, frustrated photographers and journalists, including many women, vowed to do better in the future.

REPORTING OPERATION IRAQI FREEDOM

After the difficulties that reporters experienced in covering Operation Desert Storm, what could they expect in the next Gulf conflict? Fortunately, history did not repeat itself in the case of war reporting.

For Operation Iraqi Freedom, the U.S. military allowed six hundred reporters to be embedded with the troops in the field. In previous U.S. wars, reporters had been prevented from covering the action near the front lines. In the second Gulf War, reporters handled lifesaving equipment in addition to their microphones, cameras, and other reporting gear as they traveled with the troops.

For the first time in history, the Pentagon drafted an agreement with both national and international media bureau chiefs to give journalists unprecedented access to daily combat operations in Iraq. The agreement also promised that minimal restrictions would be placed on embedded journalists.[8] One of the factors that motivated the Pentagon to allow embedded journalists was Saddam Hussein himself. According to Bryan Whitman, the deputy assistant secretary of defense for public affairs and one of the coauthors of the plan:

> *Our potential adversary was a practiced liar, who used deception to fool the world community about what he was up to. . . . We believed by putting a trained observer in the field—which I think is the definition of a reporter—to report in near real time, we could counter some of the disinformation coming out of the Iraqi Ministry of Defense.*[11]

The world would soon learn exactly how outrageous some of the claims made by the Iraqi Ministry of Defense could be. On April 4, even after U.S. troops had seized Saddam International Airport, Mohammed Saeed al-Sahhaf, the Iraqi information minister, continued his claims on television that Iraq was

MOLLY BINGHAM, PHOTOGRAPHER

JOURNALIST

When six heavily armed Iraqi men ordered photographer Molly Bingham to leave the Palestine Hotel with them on March 25, 2003, she was frightened and didn't want to leave the safety of the hotel. One look at their weapons, however, gave her little choice but to obey the command.

Bingham, aged thirty-four, had been staying with other Western journalists at the hotel.

Working on an assignment for the World Picture News Photo Agency, she was sent to Iraq to photograph the effects of war on Iraqi citizens. Bingham had no idea why the Iraqi government would want to interrogate her.

For the previous nine years, the award-winning photographer had been covering the plight of downtrodden people victimized by various global conflicts. Her work had taken her to far-off places such as Rwanda, Burundi, and Afghanistan. She had taken a brief two-and-a-half-year break to work as former Vice President Al Gore's official photographer.

As the armed men sped away in a car with Bingham, she was told: "We're taking you to a very, very safe place . . . and we'll have a surprise for you. Maybe a good surprise, maybe a bad surprise. I don't know."[9] That "safe" place turned out to be the notorious Abu Ghraib Prison. Known for the brutal torture of its prisoners, it was the largest prison in the Arab world.

At the prison, Bingham joined two U.S. journalists, a Danish photographer, and a peace activist who also had been taken prisoner. Bingham was taken into an interrogation room where she was accused of being an American spy. She was repeatedly asked about her connections to the Pentagon and CIA, although Bingham explained that she was simply a photographer on assignment.

Bingham and the four other detainees were put in separate cells. At night, they could hear screams and other horrifying sounds as prisoners were being tortured. Bingham hid under her blanket one night as a prisoner was beaten outside her cell door. She was afraid that she would be killed if the guards saw her looking at the horrifying scene.

There were other terrifying sounds. Each day, Bingham could hear the roar of coalition fighter jets flying over the compound. The windows rattled as bombs exploded nearby. Bingham wondered whether the prison itself would soon be hit by a bomb.

On the seventh day of her captivity, Bingham was brought back to the interrogation room. The main interrogator told her, "The judge has made a decision. You kill."[10] As Bingham began to plead for her life, the man's lip curled in a sneer. It had been a mean-spirited joke; Bingham was not going to be executed. In fact, she and the other four Westerners were going to be released. The Iraqi officials never explained why the five had been arrested or why they were going to be released. The group was split up into two minivans and driven to Iraq's border with Jordan.

In Jordan, the journalists were able to call their worried loved ones to tell them of their release. Bingham's overjoyed father, Barry Bingham Jr., later commented that he hoped his daughter would take up a safer line of work, such as fashion photography. Upon hearing her father's wishes, Bingham laughed and said: "I don't think I'm particularly good at that, so I'll try to stick to the things I know how to do well."[12]

winning the war. He went so far as to state that Americans had captured the airport, only to be chased out by brave Iraqi soldiers.

The proposal to embed journalists was risky for both the military and the media. The last time the military had allowed reporters unrestricted access to the war was in Vietnam, where their coverage helped to bring down a president. There was also risk on the part of the reporters. In addition to the physical dangers of traveling with the troops, there was also the danger that they would lose credibility. Would this close relationship with the military compromise their objectivity? Fortunately, the decision to have embedded reporters was mostly successful for both sides.[13]

Veteran ABC reporter Ted Koppel called the plan to embed journalists with frontline units a "reporter's dream."[14] Koppel made this announcement in the middle of a blinding sandstorm as he struggled to maintain a grasp on his microphone. Katherine M. Skiba of the *Milwaukee Journal Sentinel* shared his excitement over being in the midst of the action. Embedded with the 101st Airborne Division's aviation brigade, Skiba said that working as an embedded journalist was like "sitting on the front seat of history."[15]

Although the coverage by embedded journalists was often restricted to the narrow vantage point of the activities of their unit, their observations of U.S. troops during combat revealed a dramatic portrait of well-trained and highly disciplined soldiers. The reporters also witnessed firsthand the bravery and dedication of the troops. Skiba said that she was extremely impressed by the dedication of her brigade's executive officer when he calmly wrote his blood type on his flak jacket before heading out to the front lines.

BREAKING THE RULES

Although embedded journalists had been granted unprecedented access in their war coverage, they were required to obey certain restrictions. For example, embedded journalists were not allowed to reveal details of troop operations or locations that could compromise missions, especially those that were time-sensitive. Journalists were also prohibited from revealing classified information. And finally, journalists were prohibited from using photographs of enemy POWs, including their faces, name tags, or other identifying features. If journalists disobeyed any of these restrictions, their placement could be terminated.

In a highly publicized incident, reporter Geraldo Rivera was kicked out of Iraq for revealing troop maneuvers to television audiences. The military was angered when Rivera paused in his report to hunker down in the sand and trace a map of troop movements with his finger. Because the Iraqi military could easily have been watching this news segment, Rivera had put the lives of these troops in danger by revealing details of a covert mission on air.

But Rivera was not the only reporter to be booted out of Iraq for violating the Pentagon's restrictions. Cheryl Diaz Meyer lost her position with the Marines' Second Tank Battalion when one of her photographs ran on the front page of the *Dallas Morning News*. Meyer had taken a compelling photograph of an Iraqi detainee being strip-searched by U.S. Marines. (The Iraqi was later released.) The editors of the newspaper pulled Meyer from her embedded position before she could be terminated by the military. She spent the rest of the war pursuing stories independently in Baghdad.

FEMBEDS

Covering the war as an embedded journalist was a positive experience for most of the women reporting in the field. Out of the six hundred journalists embedded in the second Gulf War, sixty were female. During the war, the female embeds earned the nickname "fembeds." Although fembeds were eager to cover the war, some female reporters believed that the Pentagon wasn't assigning women to units that were heading to the front lines. According to CNN's Lisa Rose Weaver, "All the women embeds, and there weren't very many of them, were with things like helicopter units and air units." Few women journalists were embedded with frontline combat troops, so they were unable to report on direct fighting.

The Pentagon, however, laid the blame on the news organizations. According to spokesman Major Tim Blair, who managed the embedding program, the military never asked reporters who wished to be embedded to write their gender on their applications. He claims that the news agencies chose which reporters they wanted to embed, and most picked male reporters. That statement would have been of little comfort to Lyndsey Layton of the *Washington Post*. Embedded on the U.S.S. *Abraham Lincoln*, she never saw combat or bonded with troops. She was concerned that while 10 percent of the embedded reporters in Iraq were women, one third of the embeds on the carrier were female. Layton noted in exasperation, "Someone told me that aircraft carriers were for girls . . . which made me kind of mad."

Lisa Rose Weaver spent the start of the war as an embedded journalist with the 52nd Air Defense Artillery Brigade in northern Kuwait. She said that it took about a week for the male troops to feel comfortable around her. Initially, female embeds encountered what Weaver called the "ma'am factor."

Male soldiers were often extremely polite to female civilians, referring to them as "ma'am" instead of by their first names.

Female reporters initially worried that this formality would prevent them from gaining good stories from the troops. Ann Scott Tyson of the *Christian Science Monitor,* however, thought that the ma'am factor worked as an asset for her. "People aren't going to put on the same

CNN's Lisa Weaver reported from her embedded position with the 52nd Air Defense Artillery Brigade.

sort of tough veneer or the sort of more macho side that they may feel they have to hold up to another man. It could help being a woman—as long as you're not a wimp. As long as you go with the flow, [and] you don't ask for special treatment." As Tyson soon discovered, however, once the troops faced the stress of enemy fire, the ma'am factor was the first thing to go.

After a few initial rough patches, Weaver was able to bond with the troops in her unit. "When they figured out I was going to stay—especially when they saw a CBS crew of three men drop out when things were getting kind of weird and I stayed—that definitely boosted my ratings with them. . . . And once they figured out I wasn't into doing stories that just made them look bad and that I wasn't just digging into people's personal lives, then they were OK with it." The troops became so comfortable with Weaver's presence that they were unfazed when she reported on a friendly fire incident in which her unit accidentally shot down a U.S. jet.

As the Patriot antimissile unit she was embedded with traveled into central Iraq, Weaver experienced the dangers of warfare. Mortar shells rained down

In April 2003, CNN's Jane Araf reports live from an area in northern Iraq controlled by Kurdish fighters. It was formerly controlled by the Iraqi regime.

along the road during the convoy's five-day trek. The unit was forced to travel on sandy roads because a nearby highway was not considered to be safe. Many of the heavier vehicles became trapped in the sand. The dust from a sandstorm disoriented many of the troops, causing some to drive off the road. Weaver reported that in contrast to the warm welcome some Iraqis showed troops along the roadway, two units heading north were caught in firefights as they neared small towns. According to Sergeant Cara Williams of Weaver's unit: "The worst part of the drive is coming up to the built-up areas. I think we felt a little anxious, just trying to make sure nobody went out where they weren't supposed to."

Despite certain advantages of working as an embedded journalist, not all reporters covering the war chose to be embedded. Some journalists, referred to as "unilateral" reporters, struck out on their own, often at great personal danger. They believed that a broader journalistic perspective needed to be added to the war coverage.

AT THE END OF THE STORY

The decision to have embedded journalists was not a complete success for everyone. Embedded journalists faced the same dangers from the enemy as did the troops. Michael Kelly, a reporter for the *Boston Globe*, was the first embedded American journalist to die in the war. He had been traveling with the Army's 3rd Infantry Division. Three other journalists were taken captive by the Iraqi government, although they were later released. A total of eleven journalists died in the three-week war.

Was the war a complete success for the women journalists who covered it? Veteran reporter Denby Fawcett, who slogged through jungles to cover the Vietnam War, states: "My feeling is that this wasn't really a war for women in terms of getting out and being at the heart of the matter. It wasn't a great war in terms of women really proving themselves." Although Fawcett believes that women reporters still have more progress to make on the battlefield, she is convinced that they have already proven to be capable of the challenge.

THE CHALLENGE OF REBUILDING IRAQ

CHAPTER SEVEN

> "Women in combat is not about equality or equal opportunity. The point is national Security. . . . Some of the best and most capable are women."
>
> **• U.S. Representative Heather Wilson,
> a retired Air Force officer and the
> only female veteran in Congress**

After President Bush declared an end to Operation Iraqi Freedom on May 1, 2003, the United States faced the formidable challenge of running postwar Iraq. The war was won, but the United States faced what might be an even bigger hurdle—winning the peace. It is a challenge that has been deadly for many U.S. soldiers. A year and a half after the war officially ended, over 1,400 U.S. troops had lost their lives in Iraq. And the number of casualties continues to climb. By contrast, 147 U.S. troops were killed in the first Gulf War in 1991. Most U.S. casualties in the second Gulf War occurred after the official end of the war. This trend does not bode well for U.S. troops stationed in Iraq in the years to come.

FALL OF A DICTATOR

Unlike the first Persian Gulf War, Operation Iraqi Freedom destroyed Saddam Hussein's regime and drove him from power. For several months, the fallen leader was forced to hide in a different place each night to avoid capture. Hussein

Soon after the war ended, Iraqis such as this girl named Leila moved into makeshift houses at garbage dumps. These families make their living by collecting plastic items to sell to recycling factories and raising livestock that feed off the food found in the dump.

suffered a serious blow on July 22, when his sons, Uday and Qusay, were killed by U.S troops in a fierce firefight in the northern city of Mosul. The two brothers had been holed up in a villa. Acting on a tip, U.S. troops surrounded the house and began exchanging gunfire. The gunfight was so fierce that it shredded the very walls that were providing the brothers cover.

After several months on the run, Suddam Hussein was captured by U.S. troops on December 13, 2003. The ruthless dictator was found on a sheep farm across the Tigris River from some of his opulent palaces. Hussein was discovered cowering in a hole in the ground underneath a mud shack. When captured, Hussein's appearance was unkempt and his behavior disoriented.[1] The man who had urged his country's citizens to fight U.S. soldiers to the death meekly surrendered without a fight.

FROM CHEERS TO JEERS

The United States had promised Iraqis a democratic form of government once Hussein was removed from power. However, it is proving to be difficult to get the country functioning again and to build a democracy in a country that has endured decades of repression. The people need to be fed. The streets need to be patrolled. The country's oil industry needs to be up and running. A new Iraqi government must be put in place of the old regime.

Strong anti-Americanism had surfaced in Iraq. The cheers of welcome had turned into jeers for the coalition troops. The Shiites in the south began to challenge the U.S. presence in Iraq within weeks of the fall of Hussein's regime. In 2004, insurgents across Iraq began a campaign of bombings and other attacks on local officials and coalition troops. As civilians entered Iraq either as journalists, relief workers, or construction workers, they became targets for the insurgents. People from many different countries besides the United States have been kidnapped by rebel forces. The militants demand that foreign governments withdraw their forces from Iraq. Some of the kidnap victims have been released; others have been brutally beheaded by insurgents who videotaped their grisly deeds.

The gruesome beheading of U.S. businessman Nick Berg was in retaliation for the abuse of Iraqi prisoners by U.S. soldiers at the Abu Ghraib prison. Once the most brutal prison in Iraq under Hussein's leadership, Abu Ghraib became the site of further atrocities in early 2004, but this time committed by U.S troops. It was a blemish on an otherwise brave and exemplary service record shown by U.S. troops fighting in Iraq. Male and female soldiers stationed at the facility were accused of mistreating Iraqi prisoners of war. These soldiers were removed from duty as soon as the abuses became public. Some faced court martial and the possibility of serving prison terms for their actions.[2]

WHERE ARE THE WEAPONS?

In his State of the Union Address on January 28, 2003, President George Bush made his case to the American people for going to war with Iraq. In his speech, Bush claimed that Hussein was a danger to American security because he possessed weapons of mass destruction. Based on information gathered by British intelligence sources, the president stated that Iraq had attempted to purchase large quantities of uranium from Africa. These actions would signal that Iraq might already have nuclear weapon capability. Based on this threat, the president urged that the United States wage a pre-emptive war against Iraq.

During Operation Iraqi Freedom, U.S. troops searched for these weapons of mass destruction. None were found. Debate began to swirl over the validity of the information that the White House received. According to Charles Duelfer, the chief U.S. weapons inspector in Iraq, Hussein's stockpiles of weapons had been destroyed years before the United States invaded Iraq in 2003. The absence of weapons of mass destruction greatly weakened the United States' original reason for engaging in war with Iraq.[3]

But one fact remains clear: Despite the current controversies over the justification for going to war, the brave men and women who answered the call of duty conducted themselves with courage and conviction. And once again, women proved their rightful place in the modern U.S. Army.

A female soldier guards the scene in Mosul where U.S. troops held a six-hour gun battle resulting in the deaths of Hussein's sons Uday and Qusay on July 22, 2003.

TIMELINE

July 25, 1990	Hussein meets with U.S. ambassador to Iraq, April C. Glaspie.
August 2, 1990	Iraq invades Kuwait. UN Security Council condemns the invasion.
August 3, 1990	League of Arab States condemns the invasion. It demands Iraq's withdrawal from Kuwait.
August 6, 1990	UN Security Council, at the urging of British prime minister Margaret Thatcher, passes Resolution 661, which establishes an embargo against Iraq. Iraq reacts by annexing Kuwait.
August 9, 1990	First U.S. ground troops arrive in Saudi Arabia to participate in Operation Desert Shield. Journalists begin to arrive in large numbers, 10 percent of whom are women.
August 23, 1990	Hussein appears on television with some of his captives.
November 29, 1990	UN Security Council authorizes the use of force against Iraq unless it withdraws its troops from Kuwait by January 15, 1991. U.S. troops continue to gather in Saudi Arabia.
January 17, 1991	Air war against Iraq begins. Iraq attempts to break up the coalition by attacking Israel with Scud missiles.
January 18, 1991	President George H. W. Bush authorizes the call-up of one million National Guard members and reservists.
January 21, 1991	Lieutenant Phoebe Jeter becomes the war's first female Scudbuster.
January 25, 1991	Iraq creates an oil slick in the Persian Gulf.
January 31, 1991	Iraqi soldiers capture the first female prisoner of war, Melissa Rathbun-Nealy.
February 22, 1991	Iraqis ignite approximately 500 oil wells in Kuwait.
February 24, 1991	The ground war begins. Medical teams consisting of men and women follow behind the troops.

February 27, 1991	Major Rhonda Cornum joins a rescue mission. She is captured by the Iraqis.
February 28, 1991	A cease-fire is declared and the fighting ends.
March 17, 1991	First U.S. troops depart for home.
September 11, 2001	Terrorist attacks on the Pentagon and World Trade Center kill around 3,000 people on U.S. soil.
January 29, 2002	In his first State of the Union address, President George W. Bush calls Iraq, along with North Korea and Iran, an "axis of evil." These comments are the first of many on the part of the White House favoring U.S. action against Iraq.
October 16, 2002	President Bush signs Iraq war resolution.
November 8, 2002	UN weapons inspections resume after a four-year lapse.
March 17, 2003	President Bush sends an ultimatum to Saddam Hussein and his sons to leave Iraq within forty-eight hours or else face military conflict with the United States.
March 20, 2003	Ground war of Operation Iraqi Freedom begins at 8 P.M. EST.
March 21, 2003	First U.S. casualties of war occur.
March 23, 2003	The 507th Maintenance Battalion is ambushed near city of Nasiriyah.
April 1, 2003	Private First Class Jessica Lynch is rescued from an Iraqi hospital by a Special Operations team.
April 5, 2003	U.S. tanks roll into Baghdad and take over the capital city.
April 11, 2003	U.S. military holds a memorial service for Private First Class Lori Piestewa and the other six soldiers of the 507th killed in the ambush near Nasiriyah.
April 13, 2003	Private First Class Shoshana Johnson and six other POWs are found alive in a house outside of Tikrit.
May 1, 2003	President George W. Bush declares an end to major combat in Iraq.
July 22, 2003	Saddam Hussein's sons and henchmen, Uday and Qusay, are killed after a six-hour gunfight with U.S. soldiers.
December 13, 2003	Saddam Hussein is captured by U.S. troops. He is found hiding in an underground hole on a farm near Tikrit.

SOURCE NOTES

Introduction

1. "Saving Private Lynch," a *Bill Kurtis Special Report*, A&E Channel, May 11, 2003.
2. Cathy Booth Thomas, "Taken by Surprise," *Time*, April 7, 2003, p. 64.
3. Thomas, p. 64
4. Thomas, p. 64.
5. Jerry Adler, "Jessica's Liberation," *Newsweek*, April 14, 2003, p. 42.
6. Adler, p. 42.
7. Jamie McIntyre, "Pentagon Calls BBC's Lynch Allegations 'Ridiculous.'" [Online] Available at www.cnn.com, May 20, 2003.

CHAPTER ONE

1. James F. Dunnigan and Austin Bay, *A Quick and Dirty Guide to War* (New York: William Morrow and Company, Inc., 1996), p. 60.
2. "War in Iraq: Special Report." [Online] Available at www.tlc.discovery.com.
3. Dunnigan and Bay, p. 12.
4. Thomas B. Allen, F. Berry Clifton, and Norman Polmar. *CNN War in the Gulf* (Atlanta: Turner Publishing, Inc., 1991), p. 61.
5. Dunnigan, p. 46.
6. Jadranka Porter, *Under Siege in Kuwait: A Survivor's Story* (Boston: Houghton Mifflin Company, 1991), p. 13.
7. Porter, pp. 16, 17.

CHAPTER TWO

1. Richard Alan Schwartz, *Encyclopedia of the Persian Gulf War* (Jefferson, NC: McFarland & Company, Inc., 1998), p. 5.
2. Victoria Sherrow, *Women and the Military: An Encyclopedia* (Santa Barbara, CA: ABC-CLIO, Inc., 1996), p. 214.
3. Schwartz, p. 171.
4. "Women Who Served in War." [Online] Available at www.military-woman.org/war.htm, p. l.
5. Schwartz, p. 172.
6. David Jones, *Women Warriors: A History* (Washington: Brassey's, 1977), p. 245.

7. Maj. Gen. Jeanne Holm, *Women in the Military: An Unfinished Revolution* (Novato, CA: Presidio, 1992), p. 451.
8. Holm, p. 470.
9. Holm, p. 447.
10. Holm, p. 451.
11. Holm, p. 470.
12. William B. Breuer, *War and American Women: Heroism, Deeds, and Controversy* (Westport, CT: Praeger, 1997), p. 151.

CHAPTER THREE

1. Yossef Bodansky, *Bin Laden: The Man Who Declared War on America* (New York: Prima Publishing, 2001), p. vii.
2. The New York Times, *A Nation Challenged: A Visual History of 9/11 and Its Aftermath* (New York: Calloway, 2002), p. 30.
3. *The New York Times,* p. 26.
4. *The New York Times,* p. 44.
5. CBS News, *What We Saw* (New York: Simon & Schuster, 2002), p. 42.
6. Bodansky, p. 3.
7. *The New York Times*, p. 156.
8. Askold Krushelnycky, "Afghanistan: U.S. Commander Declares 'Operation Anaconda' Over," Radio Free Europe/Radio Liberty. [Online] Available at www.rferl.org, March 18, 2002.

CHAPTER FOUR

1. Shauna Curphey, "1 in 7 U.S. Military Personnel in Iraq is Female," Women's ENews, available at www.womensnews.org, March 22, 2003.
2. Marilyn Elias, "Mommies Marching Off to War," *USA Today*, April 8, 2003, p. 1D.
3. Lt. Gen. Claudia Kennedy, "Yer Mama Wears Combat Boots and We're Proud," *Ms. Magazine*, Available at www.msmagazine.com, Summer 2003.
4. Elaine Donnelly, "Women Soldiers Serving at Greater Risk," *Human Events*, May 19, 2003, p. 8.
5. "G.I. Jane," *Current Events*, May 2, 2003, p. 3.
6. Leela Jacinto, "Girl Power." [Online] Available at www.abcnews.com, January 14, 2003.
7. Ann Scott Tyson and Liz Marlantes, "The Expanding Role of GI Jane," *Christian Science Monitor*, April 3, 2003, p.1.
8. NBC News, "Operation Iraqi Freedom," Discovery Channel.
9. Kennedy.

10. Elias.
11. Nancy Gibbs and others, "An American Family Goes to War," *Newsweek*, March 24, 2003, pp. 27–35.
12. Gibbs, p. 27.
13. "Women at War: The First Woman to . . .," *Glamour*, June 2003, p. 178.
14. "Women at War: The First Woman to . . ."
15. NBC News.

CHAPTER FIVE

1. Elizabeth Kassner, *Desert Storm Journal: A Nurse's Story* (Lincoln Center, MA: The Cottage Press, 1993), p. 32.
2. Maj. Gen. Jeanne Holm, *Women in the Military: An Unfinished Revolution* (Novato, CA: Presidio, 1992), p. 442.
3. Kassner, p. 54.
4. Holm, p. 458.
5. Kassner, p. 88.
6. "U.S. to Screen Troops Returning from Iraq," Midwest Television, Inc., June 2, 2003, [Online] Available at www.kfmb.com.
7. Janet Boivin, R.N., "Floating Hospital a Welcome Berth for War Wounded," *Nursing Spectrum*, April 1, 2003. Available at community.nursingspectrum.com.
8. Boivin.
9. Scott Cannon, "Doctors, Nurses Treat War Casualties in Makeshift Hospital," *The Kansas City Star*, March 29, 2003, www.web19.epnet.com.
10. Cannon.
11. Cannon.
12. Cannon.
13. Boivin.

CHAPTER SIX

1. "Christiane Amanpour's RTNDA 2000 Speech," [Online] Available at www.unf.edu/jaxmedia/amanpour.htm, p. 2.
2. John J. Fialka, *Hotel Warriors: Covering the Gulf War* (Washington: The Woodrow Wilson Center Press, 1991), p. 19.
3. Fialka, p. 19.
4. Molly Moore, *A Woman at War: Storming Kuwait with the U.S. Marines* (New York: Charles Scribner's Sons, 1993), p. 3.
5. Moore, p. 3.
6. Sygma photographers, *In the Eye of Desert Storm* (New York: Harry N. Abrams, Inc., 1991), p. 20.

7. Sygma photographers, p. 155.
8. Susan B Markisz. "Putting the Media in Soldiers Shoes," May 2003, The Digital Journalist. [Online] Available at www.digitaljournalist.org.
9. "Picture This: Photojournalist Tells of Her Captivity in Iraqi Prison," *20/20*, April 4, 2003, [Online] Available at www.abcnews.com.
10. Molly Bingham, "We Have Either a Good Surprise for You or a Bad Surprise . . .," *The Guardian*, April 3, 2003. [Online] Available at media.guardian.co.uk.
11. "Picture This: Photojournalist Tells of Her Captivity in Iraqi Prison."
12. Leonard R Sussman, "Embedded Journalists: The Gamble That Won," The Anniston Star, May 4, 2003. [Online] Available at www.anniston-star.com.
13. Markisz.
14. Sussman.
15. Spc. Bill Putnam, "Embedded Journalists Recount Tales of Crowds, Dedication," May 2003, Defense Technical Information Center, [Online] Available at www.dtic.mil.
16. Markisz.
17. Markisz.
18. Brian Braiker, "'Fembeds' Reflect on Covering War," *Newsweek* Web exclusive, May 16, 2003. [Online] Available at www.msnbc.com.
19. Braiker.
20. Braiker.
21. Braiker.
22. Braiker.
23. Lisa Rose Weaver, "Dangerous Drive into Iraq," *CNN News*, March 26, 2003. [Online] Available at www.cnn.com.
24. Braiker.

CHAPTER SEVEN

1. "Saddam 'Caught Like a Rat' in a Hole," *CNN News,* December 15, 2003. [Online] Available at www.cnn.com.
2. "Abuse of Iraqi Prisoners Probed," *60 Minutes,* April 28, 2004. [Online] Available at www.cbs.news.
3. Dana Priest and Walter Pincus, "U.S. 'Almost All Wrong" on Weapons," *Washington Post,* October 7, 2004.

BIBLIOGRAPHY

Allen, Thomas B., F. Berry Clifton, and Norman Polmar. *CNN War in the Gulf*. Atlanta: Turner Publishing, 1991.

Blacksmith, E.A., editor. *Women in the Military*. New York: H.W. Wilson Company, 1992.

Bodansky, Yossef. *Bin Laden: The Man Who Declared War on America*. New York: Prima Publishing, 2001.

Breuer, William B. *War and American Women: Heroism, Deeds, and Controversy*. Westport, CT: Praeger, 1997.

CBS Worldwide, Inc. *What We Saw*. New York: Simon & Schuster, 2002.

"Christiane Amanpour's RTNDA 2000 Speech." Available at www.unf.edu/jaxmedia/amanpour.htm.

Cornum, Rhonda, as told to Peter Copeland. *She Went to War: The Rhonda Cornum Story*. Novato, CA: Presidio Press, 1992.

Dorr, Robert F. *Desert Shield: The Build-Up: The Complete Story*. Osceola, WI: Motorbooks International, 1991.

Dunnigan, James F., and Austin Bay. *A Quick and Dirty Guide to War*. New York: William Morrow and Company, 1996.

Fialka, John J. *Hotel Warriors: Covering the Gulf War*. Washington: The Woodrow Wilson Center Press, 1991.

Franke, Linda Bird. *Ground Zero: The Gender Wars in the Military*. New York: Simon & Schuster, 1997.

Franker, Major Thomas R. *Desert Storm Heroes: The Families at Home*. Pittsburgh: Dorrance Publishing, 1992.

Grossman, Mark. *Encyclopedia of the Persian Gulf War.* Santa Barbara, CA: ABC-CLIO, 1995.

Hiro, Dilip. *Desert Shield to Desert Storm: The Second Gulf War.* New York: Routledge, 1992.

Hirschman, Loree Draude. *She's Just Another Navy Pilot; An Aviator's Sea Journal.* Annapolis, MD: Naval Institute Press, 2000.

Holm, Maj. Gen. Jeanne. *Women in the Military: An Unfinished Revolution. Rev. ed.* Novato, CA: Presidio, 1992.

Huffman, Karen Kirk. *Living the Nightmare: Escape from Kuwait.* Lincoln, NE: Dageforde, 1999.

"IWMF's 1990 Courage in Journalism Awardees."
Available at www.iwmf.org/courage/90award.htm.

Jones, David E. *Women Warriors: A History.* Washington: Brassey's, 1997.

Kassner, Elizabeth. *Desert Storm Journal: A Nurse's Story.* Lincoln Center, MA: The Cottage Press, 1993.

Levitas, Mitchell. *A Nation Challenged: A Visual History of 9/11 and Its Aftermath.* New York: Henry Holt & Company, 2002.

Lockwood, Glenda. *Diary of a Human Shield.* London: Bloomsbury, 1991.

Makiya, Kanan. *Cruelty and Silence: War, Tyranny, Uprising, and the Arab World.* New York: W.W. Norton & Company, 1993.

Moore, Molly. *A Woman at War: Storming Kuwait with the U.S. Marines.* New York: Charles Scribner's Sons, 1993.

Picou, Carol H. "Living with Gulf War Syndrome."
Available at www.iacenter.org/depleted/picou.htm.

Porter, Jadranka. *Under Siege in Kuwait: A Survivor's Story.* Boston: Houghton Mifflin Company, 1991.

Reeve, Simon. *The New Jackals.* Boston: Northeastern University Press, 1999.

Schwartz, Richard Alan. *Encyclopedia of the Persian Gulf War.* Jefferson, N.C.: McFarland & Company, 1998.

Sherrow, Victoria. *Women and the Military: An Encyclopedia.* Santa Barbara, CA: ABC-CLIO, 1996.

Spears, Sally. *Call Sign Revlon: The Life and Death of Navy Fighter Pilot Kara Hultgreen.* Annapolis, MD: Naval Institute Press, 1998.

Sygma photographers. *In the Eye of Desert Storm.* New York: Harry N. Abrams, 1991.

Talbott, Strobe, and Nayan Chanda, eds., *The Age of Terror: America and the World After September 11.* New York: Basic Books, 2001.

Thatcher, Margaret. *The Downing Street Years.* New York: HarperCollins, 1993.

USA Today staff. *Desert Warriors: The Men and Women Who Won the Gulf War.* New York: Pocket Books, 1991.

"WIPI Features From Abroad—Kuwait."
Available at www.WomenInPhotography.org.

FURTHER READING

Although the first Persian Gulf War was short, a surprising number of books, including several for young adults, have been written about the conflict. For more information about the war itself, check out *Persian Gulf War* by Kathlyn Gay and Martin Gay (Twenty-First Century Books, 1996), *The War Against Iraq* by Don Nardo (Lucent, 2001), and *The Persian Gulf War: "The Mother of All Battles"* by Zachary Kent (Enslow, 1994). To learn about the controversies surrounding U.S. involvement in the Persian Gulf region, read *Iraq* by editors William Dudley and Stacey L. Tripp (Greenhaven Press, 1991), and *Iraq: Old Land, New Nation in Conflict* by William Spencer (Twenty-First Century Bookss, 2000).

The issue of women serving in combat roles in the military has been riddled with controversy. To learn more about this issue, read *Women in Combat: The Battle for Equality* by Richard Worth (Enslow, 1999). To learn more about female war correspondents, read *Journalists at Risk: Reporting America's Wars* by George Sullivan (Twenty-First Century Books, 2004).

The use of chemical and biological weapons was a major concern during both wars. To learn more about this issue, read *Silent Death: Biological and Chemical Terrorism* by Kathlyn Gay (Twenty-First Century Books, 2001) and *Chemical & Biological Weapons in Our Times* by Herbert M. Levine (Franklin Watts, 2001).

The Internet is a vast resource of information about current national and world news. Most major televisions stations and newspapers (for example, *www.newyorktimes.com*) maintain Web sites that contain the latest coverage of news events. To read current reports about world events written by CNN reporters, visit *www.cnn.com*. To read coverage of national and world events written especially for students, visit *www.timeforkids.com*. Students interested in reading up-to-date military reports about Operation Iraqi Freedom can visit the Web site of the United States Central Command at *www.centcom.mil*. To take fun-filled quizzes and play word games based on a current events topic, students may visit *www.eduplace.com/ss/current*.

INDEX